T0129627

ENDORSEMENTS

"Everyone has a life story to tell of his or her own that intertwines their events with God's own love story. This book is one of those where through seemingly ordinary days we see glimpses of God, sacred moments, in which the Eternal orchestrates His wonderful love story. I hope that walking through these pages will bring to your mind and heart how well the Lord Jesus Christ has also loved you."

Carolyn Crandall Hays,
women's Bible teacher,
Chattanooga, Tennessee

"Dennis Fox's autobiography inspires one to stick with his dreams and desires despite any obstacles. His memories and experiences that he shares throughout the book are enjoyable and relatable."

Lynn Weaver,
nurse and member of Saint Angela Merici Catholic Church,
Fairview Park, Ohio

"I read Dennis Fox's *Born to Serve* autobiography and found it inspiring and professionally informative. It can give the reader hope if depressed, insecure, concerned about the future, lift one up, and can prove that the Lord can open doors of opportunity as it did for him, even though life was not always a bed of roses. Many victories, however, were won by God's grace."

Norma Okuma,
former nurse in the Lakewood City School District in Lakewood,
Ohio

Dennis Fox's autobiography shows what can be accomplished through life, experiences. As a youngster, he had little self-confidence but determination and faith in God led him to attain a successful teaching career in English and music.

Ken Kalina
Retired Cleveland School Teacher, Member St. Teresa of Avila Parish
in Sheffield Village, Ohio

"If you want proof that God works in the lives of people, *Born to Serve* is it. The autobiography of Dennis Fox proves that when someone is surrendered to God and willing to leave all the choices to Him, his life will undoubtedly bring glory to Christ!"

Pastor Gregory A. Davis,
Southwest Baptist Church,
Brunswick, Ohio

"'The steps of a good man are ordered by the Lord' (Psalm 37:23). This book tells the story of a good man whose steps were, and continue to be, ordered by the Lord. It is the hope of the author that the experiences he shares within these pages will point the lost to our Savior and challenge Christians to yield to the work of the Holy Spirit in their lives. You will be inspired when you read what God can do through a surrendered servant!"

Joyce Witzke,
Cleveland Baptist Church,
Cleveland, Ohio

"As a colleague, watching Dennis Fox teach over the years, I have been able to observe his passion in educating and expanding the knowledge of his students. There is a lot to be gained by reading his life story. It can inspire all to learn, live and persevere."

Pamela V. Craig,
Second Missionary Baptist Church, Cleveland, Ohio,
retired Cleveland School teacher

"I have had the pleasure of personally knowing Dennis Fox. He is an amazing person and his autobiography is a testament to that! I enjoyed reading about his entire life but was especially impressed reading about his childhood."

Brian Will,
Construction worker in the Cleveland area

Mr. Fox's book is an encouragement for all ages taking us through his trials and tribulations and directs us to his present day success. How he illustrates that Jesus Christ has a plan for every believer who is willing to allow Him to lead impressed me the most!

Pastor Paul Males, Jr.,
Westlake Baptist Church,
Westlake, Ohio

BORN to SERVE

Dennis R. Fox

WESTBOW
PRESS®
A DIVISION OF THOMAS NELSON
& ZONDERVAN

WestBow Press books may be ordered through booksellers or by contacting:

WestBow Press
A Division of Thomas Nelson & Zondervan
1663 Liberty Drive
Bloomington, IN 47403
www.westbowpress.com
1 (866) 928-1240

ISBN: 978-1-5127-1987-1 (sc)
ISBN: 978-1-5127-1989-5 (hc)
ISBN: 978-1-5127-1988-8 (e)

Library of Congress Control Number: 2015918863

Print information available on the last page.

WestBow Press rev. date: 12/29/2015

My baby picture

AUTOBIOGRAPHY

Dennis R. Fox
In my childhood days, I believed I was
Ugly, Insecure, Frustrated, Defeated,
Had low self-esteem and was bullied,
But thankfully God altered my thinking.

CONTENTS

DEDICATION

I dedicate this book to the Lord, who gave me the skills to assimilate the content; my parents; my late wife, Joyce; my brother, Norman; my brothers- and sisters-in law, Dale, Carolyn, and Pauline; my children Michael, Jeffery, and Lori; my daughters-in-law, Aubrey and Kristie; my grandchildren, Abbey and Kayla; my; step grandchild Isaac, retired pastor and pastor of the Westlake Baptist Church of Westlake, Ohio; Paul Males Sr., Paul Males Jr., and their wives Virgie and Christine; the congregation of the Westlake Baptist Church; those who gave acknowledgments; and my many friends.

INTRODUCTION

In every society there are multitudes that let a failure or failures crush their ego and ultimately convince themselves that they really are ignorant. As a youngster I believed that I was not very intelligent, but the longer I lived, I became more aware that it was a fallacy. Things both negative and positive that occurred in my life happened for a reason. Thanks to the Lord, He provided me with the intelligence to succeed. When I was six months old, a seizure occurred which could have caused double vision and perhaps a memory problem, but thanks to the God of salvation and medical research, most of those maladies were eliminated. Thankfully, I did not succumb to negative dealings all of my life. Proof of that was that I graduated from high school, earned three degrees, taught English and music for over thirty years, taught piano, directed church choirs, been a pianist and organist, written and published gospel songs and choral arrangements, and written over two hundred religious and secular poems. People that I have met and directions and occurrences in my life were not accidental, for I believe in Divine intervention, and as one reads this book, I trust that he will believe that God has a purpose for all who put their faith and trust in Jesus Christ and that He will lead one in every aspect of life if God's Word is one's teacher. I thank Him that I was changed by His redeeming grace. I would think that no matter how intelligent one has been throughout life, there must have been occasions when one felt a lack of confidence, considered himself a failure, or did not have any hope for the future or even eternity. Perhaps this book could be the encouragement and answer that is needed.

I have decided to share my life's experiences because I know that many have had similar negative beliefs and have not been sure of eternity. By reading these pages, I wish all will realize that God has a niche for His children. There are those who believe that all humanity are God's children. We are all God's creation, but the Word of God totally disputes that all are His children. That comes by accepting His Son,

Jesus Christ, as his personal Savior. The Bible says in John 3:3, "Except a man be born again, he cannot see the Kingdom of God."

My niche for my life was not determined until after I was twenty-seven years of age. As I look back over the first twenty-six years of my life, I am cognizant that there were major incidences and people who had impacted the directions I chose. Therefore, I know that God has been the answer to the outcomes throughout my entire life. Even though I have failed Him at times, He has truly been my inspiration.

Life is full of twists and turns, and some might call those encounters "coincidental" or "accidental." How can I call what direction I took as coincidental or accidental since God is on my side? I have often wondered where I would have gone had I taken other forks in the road. That kind of rational has no merit since He has given me so many blessings. Why would I wish it to be different? Thank God for the course that I took. I would not desire it to be any other way, because I believe I was born to serve. That serving could not be realized, however, until I became born again.

CHAPTER 1

Early Life

On December 4, 1936, at 1:30 in the afternoon, my life began at Good Samaritan Hospital in Lebanon, Pennsylvania, about twenty-seven miles east of Harrisburg and fifteen miles east of Hershey Amusement Park. Next to the park is where Hershey candy was made.

My first teeth

For the first three years of my life, my family lived in two locations. Then my parents bought property and built and lived in a sixteen-square-foot garage in Avon Heights, a mile east of Lebanon. We lived in that garage for two years while Dad, who was very skilled in carpentry, designed, and with no assistance, built a two-story house on that land.

That house
Notice the antique automobile in front of the house.

I got my first haircut when I was about a year old. How gross it was to have to look at the well-used spittoon in that building! The structure still exists.

The barbershop

My brother, Norman, was born in 1940. The first recollection I have of him was when my mother fell with him in her arms. Fortunately, they were not hurt.

Norman on the left, me on the right

Folks didn't have the modern conveniences of the twenty-first century, especially if living in a rural area as we did. We had electricity, but we didn't have running water until after World War II. Our bathroom was a creaking, wooden, spider-infested outhouse. How awful that was in the horribly cold winters! For bathing, we had to hand pump water into a dishpan from an outside well and heat it on a coal stove.

The house was also heated by coal. Excitement swelled within me whenever the huge coal trucks backed up to our basement window. I watched the tons of coal slide down a metal ramp through the opened window and into the furnace room.

To save heat in the winter, we kept it confined to the first floor. Dad draped a wool blanket at the top of the steps, where our bedrooms were located. My bedroom got so cold, I could actually see my breath. Jack Frost painted beautiful designs on the windows. I crawled under a wool blanket, and eventually my body heat warmed my spot in the bed.

With no insulated walls, the situation was just as horrible in the summer. There were times during July and August when we slept in the living room, just inside the open front door, wishing for temperatures a bit cooler. The *Lebanon Daily News* listed the dates when the temperature would rise above ninety degrees. It was not uncommon for there to be thirty or more consecutive days for us to sweat the incredible heat. It was just as common to live through winters when the temperature was below zero for weeks.

All year, a special truck delivered huge blocks of ice for our icebox. We had no refrigerator, but the ice kept the milk, meat, and other foods from spoiling. The deliveryman used an ice pick to crack the blocks of ice into the amount ordered for each house. Ice chunks fell to the street. What a thrill we neighborhood children had as we followed the ice truck, picking up dropped chunks and sucking on them until they melted! They had no taste, but it was enjoyable.

Dad built two sheds in our backyard. He raised chickens, pigeons, rabbits, and even pigs in those sheds. Perhaps one could have called us mini-farmers.

One of the sheds

4

Once the pigs were grown, he had them butchered. The hams were hung on hooks for curing, the process of aging them so they don't spoil. By hanging on hooks for about two months in a cold room, they became safe for eating. Mom canned the rest of the meat in salt brine.

Dad fed the hogs, but it was my responsibility to feed the other animals. That was not a problem, because all I had to do was spread grain across the ground. How fascinating it was to watch hundreds of chickens and ducks gobble up the grain and scatter if just a bit of noise was heard or movement sensed! Being a kid, I sometimes purposely moved or made noise just to watch them scatter.

Of course, there was a problem that caused me to tremble. Among those creatures were roosters that became upset with my presence as I spread the grain. They were very aggressive, and if I were not alert and ready to dash to freedom, they viciously attacked me with their pointed beaks.

Another problem I encountered daily involved the collection of the eggs laid in the hens' nests. They also were not appreciative of my intrusion. As I reached under their feathered bodies, they entered attack mode. My only defense was to wear gloves or cover their heads with a cloth.

Chickens

Dad owned a lot of chickens
That I had to feed without fail.
Every morning throughout the year,
I spread the grain from a pail.

As I entered the huge pen,
I walked with a sense of fear,
For those dangerous-looking roosters
Could peck me as high as my ear.

But the worst part of the task
Was gathering eggs from the hen.
She would protect her domain
And chase me away from the den.

By raising chickens and pigs and growing many vegetables, Dad supplied fresh food for the table. There was very little expense in a day when the economy was tough. I can still visualize that hatchet in his hand as it chopped off the heads of those helpless chickens. Their necks were placed on the tree stump he used as a chopping block. My brother and I had to stand far enough away not to be splattered with the blood. Fortunately, I was not expected to use the hatchet. It was an experience most children and adults will never endure.

Dad submerged the chickens in boiling water until the feathers could easily be plucked. That was the only way that procedure could be accomplished. Once the feathers were removed, Mom took over the more pleasant job of cutting up the chicken and frying the fresh meat for a scrumptious meal.

Mom was from a family of nine children and learned to cook at an early age. Pennsylvania Dutch cooking became her specialty. She really could have started her own restaurant. One of the dishes she prepared was beef heart. She cut the cooked heart into small pieces, mixed them with mashed potatoes, and finished by pouring on her homemade gravy.

Different sections of the United States have foods or sodas unique to those locations. There was a soda and two foods I enjoyed that were sold in the Lebanon, Lancaster, and Reading regions: Pennsylvania Dutch birch beer and scrapple and pig-feet jelly. One had to travel there and sample them to discover the taste and perhaps acquire a liking for them. Scrapple (scraps produced from pigs and shaped into squares) is sliced and fried like sausage or even Spam. To make it scrumptious, I poured molasses over it. Pig-feet jelly is concocted from the pig's feet. I have seen pig-feet jelly in northern Ohio grocery stores.

Not all animals we raised were for food. We also had pigeons. I'm familiar with two types of pigeons—barn and racing. Dad and Mom raised and raced racing pigeons. How much fun it was to put them in cages and transport them farther every week! This was essential for them to become accustomed to flying hundreds of miles. Daily training to fly long distances was just as important as a human athlete training to play a sport. Without a consistent training program, winning those races would never have been accomplished. Because of Mom and Dad's dedication, those birds won many races. What amazed me was that no matter how far from home they began their flight, they always beat us home! The most impressive race our pigeons won was the six hundred miles from Atlanta, Georgia, to Lebanon. Our pigeons, along with thousands of others, were transported there in semitrailers. The pigeons were released at the same time, flew in a circle until they found their bearings, and headed north. All of ours returned home even though they were caged without a view of the outside before they were released.

Amazing Pigeons

When I was living with my parents,
My dad owned many homing pigeons.
He trained them to fly long distances
By driving to faraway regions.

Each time, he put them in cages
And placed them carefully in the car.
Amazingly, after they were released,
They beat us home, no matter how far.

Weekly he entered them in races,
Which were not as far as Transylvania.
But some were over six hundred miles
From Georgia to Pennsylvania.

My father learned life wasn't easy from an early age. In the twenty-first century, minimum wage is around seven dollars an hour. When he was fourteen, he picked potatoes sunup to sundown for five cents a bushel or one dollar a day. I was born in the thirties, and for him to provide for our family had to be a challenge.

The following five years, he worked in a shirt factory. Not long after that, he landed a job working for the nut-and-bolt division of the Bethlehem Steel Corporation in Lebanon. He lugged seventy-five- to eighty-pound kegs of steel nuts and bolts until he retired. Though the work was eight hours of backbreaking labor, I never heard him complain. He showed me a dad who worked in spite of the wage or how difficult the responsibilities were.

Dad was a volunteer auxiliary policeman during World War II. Whenever there was a siren warning of a possible enemy attack, he immediately walked through our neighborhood, spotting any person or home with any kind of light. Total darkness was the absolute rule, no lighting or smoking cigarettes, no house or outside lights. Just a flicker of light could be detected from miles away. I can still hear the horrible sound of the air raid, with its high-pitched repetitions until the all-clear signal occurred. I remember where I was on that triumphant day, August 15, 1945, when the United States was declared the victor!

The Toughness of My Father and the Faithfulness of My Mother

My parents had very little money
During the years of my early childhood.
Our family during the World War years
Lived from pay to pay the best we could.

My father never finished school
And was employed at a young age.
The Bethlehem Steel Company
Hired him for a meager wage.

He labored forty hours every week
Working for the Bethlehem Steel.
Each day he'd lug eighty-pound kegs,
Which caused pain from his head to his heel.

He did not tell me for many years,
But the toil he did was very rough.
From morning until the end of day,
His muscles became ruggedly tough.

When he came home in the evening,
He did not have a single complaint.
All that his bosses told him to do
Was done, whether healthy or faint.

No fuss was made over what he earned,
Nor about the pains he *sorely* got.
As I looked upon his dirtied clothes,
I could see more than one soiled spot.

Even though the pay was not good,
He made sure food was on the table.
Mom also toiled at various jobs
And earned as much cash as she was able.

In order to conserve heat in the winter,
Dad blocked the register where I slept.
Consequently, during those bitter cold nights,
I was wrapped up in covers and from frostbite was kept.

The most important lessons
That my parents provided for me,
Was reading stories from God's Word,
And teaching truths I needed to see.

I respect Dad for his values
As I reflect upon his life.
His ideals had an impact upon me
And upon my mother-his wife.

Dad was ushered into heaven in October 2007, at the age of ninety-three, and Mom in March 2014, at the age of ninety-five.

When I was three years old, Mom and Dad made a decision that impacted my life. A friend led them to the Lord Jesus Christ. Not long after that decision, our family started to attend the First Baptist Church in Lebanon, Pennsylvania, where they became obedient by being baptized, joining that Bible-believing church, and faithfully attending Sunday school, Sunday morning and evening services, Wednesday prayer services, and evangelistic and revival meetings.

The former First Baptist Church

Youth class of 1944
I am in the second row wearing a black suit.

Our family learned that God provides for both our spiritual and physical needs. Philippians 4:19 (KJV) says, "But my God shall supply all your need according to his riches in glory by Christ Jesus." Dad really made me aware of that when he thanked the Lord for providing food before every meal. Those prayers were never lengthy, but they caused me to remember why there was food on the table. Thankfully, I never saw Mom or Dad smoke cigarettes or drink alcoholic beverages, because the day they received Christ, Dad, who smoked, tossed the cigarettes he still possessed into the garbage can. I do not believe mom ever dabbled in those nasty habits even before her conversion. She told me often that if God intended one to smoke, He would have put a smoke stack on one's head. In Romans 12:1-2 (KJV), the apostle Paul wrote, "I beseech you, therefore, brethren, by the mercies of God, that ye present your bodies a living sacrifice, holy, acceptable unto God, which is your reasonable service. And be not conformed to this world: but be ye transformed by the renewing of your mind, that ye may prove what is that good, and acceptable, and perfect will of God." They submitted to those verses with the aid of the Holy Spirit.

The late Pastor John Rheinert, our dedicated under-shepherd, expounded God's Word weekly, which I know was partially instrumental in my conversion at the age of fifteen.

First Baptist Church had a missionary conference for a week every year. During that week, Mom and Dad would invite those missionaries into our home for meals and fellowship. How thankful I am that I had the opportunity to hear some of their experiences in our home! Everyone should be so fortunate!

Not only did Mom and Dad become active in the church, but they also became very concerned about the young people in our neighborhood. Once a week, they would open our home to conduct a Bible club meeting. A High School Born-Again (HBA) associate would be the speaker and would use flannel graph pictures to illustrate the characters and stories of the Old and New Testaments to convince listeners of their need to accept Christ and live for Him.

HBA group in our yard
I am all the way to the left in the third row.

After Pastor and Mrs. Rheinert left the First Baptist Church, our family visited them in Wellington, Ohio, where their new ministerial work had begun at the Wellington First Baptist Church. To arrive there, we had to take the Pennsylvania Turnpike, which at the time ended near Pittsburgh. As we approached Pittsburgh, it appeared as though there were a developing thunderstorm. Actually, it was the smog from the steel mills. Because of the Clean Air Act, the residents of that city breathe much cleaner air today.

Since it was autumn, the folks of Wellington would rake their leaves into piles on the sides of the street and dispose of them with a match. What a smell as the smoke, which is more pleasant than burning timber, would permeate the air!

During our visit, the Rheinerts drove us to Cleveland, where I rode an escalator for the first time, and to Lorain, where I walked on the lengthy pier hundreds of feet into Lake Erie. What a blessing it was to visit them and to hear him again proclaim the truths of God's Word! Those dear folks have since gone home to be with the Lord, but their lives have left an everlasting impression on me, and I know I will see them again in glory. Only those who have received Christ can have that assurance, which is revealed so clearly by Jesus' words in John 14:1-6:

> Let not your heart be troubled: ye believe in God, believe also in me. In my Father's house are many mansions: if it were not so, I would have told you. I go to prepare a place for you. And if I go and prepare a place for you, I will come again, and receive you unto myself; that where I am, there ye may be also. And whither I go ye know, and the way ye know. Thomas saith unto him, Lord, we know not whither thou goest; and how can we know the way? Jesus saith unto him, I am the way, the truth, and the life: no man cometh unto the Father, but by me.

It was also our privilege to spend a day with a church family at the Sandy Cove Bible Conference Ground on the shore of the Chesapeake Bay in Maryland.

Our family on the left and them on the right

CHAPTER 2

Elementary School Years

As I entered the elementary school years of my life, a belief began to emerge that I was not very intelligent. That idea developed because schoolteachers and others convinced me I was mentally "slow." I assured myself that it was impossible to memorize anything of length.

Every year, I was required to memorize a four-line poem for the annual Christmas program. Terrified, I would stand before those staring eyes and recite mine, afraid that my mind would go blank. How amazing it was that such an event could petrify, frustrate, humiliate, and devastate a six-or seven-year-old youngster!

The next step in confidence destruction occurred one mile from my home in a two-room first-through-fourth-grade schoolhouse, where I began my public education. Each room had two grades with one teacher. The grotesque bathrooms and coat closets were adjacent to the classrooms. In the coat closets, I placed my metal lunch box that my mother faithfully packed with Lebanon bologna sandwiches and fruit. Lebanon bologna is still produced in Lebanon and is a smoked meat guaranteed not to spoil for weeks. Ketchup spiced up the taste. During my junior and senior years, there was a cafeteria where I bought hot food. What a relief!

The two-room schoolhouse

Weaver's Lebanon Bologna and Smoke House

The atmosphere was not the worst aspect of the four years. There was a bully in my class, and I became his target. If my eyes glanced toward him during the school day, he would raise his fists heavenward and mouth the words, "After class!" Being rather small in stature and not endowed with super physical strength, I knew what was in store for me if he could run faster than I. That was all I needed to cause me to begin to detest school and all its ramifications: reading, thinking, memorizing, testing, etc.

A yellow school bus transported me to and from school. To board the bus after school, I had to walk a lengthy alley to arrive at the bus stop. As I was walking with the gang one day to catch the bus, the agitator put his arm around me and told me we were buddies. He played me for a fool, because a few moments later, he and his buddies roughed me up.

For me to survive the daily walks to the bus stop, I knew something had to be done quickly. The custodian of the school lived a block from the school, and in sight of where the bus stop was located. When I told him of my plight, he allowed me to stay on his porch, until I saw the bus approaching. At that moment, I would dash to the waiting bus. What I actually should have done was inform the school authorities and my parents, but I believed the worst situation would come from the culprits, if I did!

Mom and Dad's first home after their wedding and
the custodian's house are both in the center.

A number of years after the attack in that alley, I had a similar feeling to what Ralphie had in the movie *The Christmas Story*, where a redheaded neighborhood bully seemed impelled to harass him unmercifully. Eventually, Ralphie could not hold back his frustration any longer and exploded into uncontrolled rage and beat the redhead into a bloody-nosed mess.

I compare that incident to a time, when a youngster not far from my home called me an embarrassing name for many months, that ultimately spread into the school. Since I was young and did not know how to cope, pressure and rage built up within me, as the heckling continued from him and others.

I no longer tolerated that abuse, and punched that neighbor in the mouth. Later, he surprisingly apologized. Ultimately, I had the opportunity to lead him to the Lord Jesus as his Savior.

After his apology, the name-calling subsided from the others involved. Later, I came to the conclusion that the best approach to that kind of abuse was to change my tactic and laugh with them. I learned, that if the one being tormented becomes embarrassed and cringes, the harassment becomes worse. Had I not let them know I was embarrassed, I would have no longer been their target.

When I was in second grade, my parents had a concern for my extracurricular in life and thought that piano lessons were for me. We had an old upright piano, which prompted them to make that decision. Perhaps they wished that would ignite a spark for me mentally, and perhaps they wished for me to experience what they did not have when they were youngsters.

A woman teacher who lived in Lebanon became my instructor. Third Street is where our church was located, and her home was located a half block west of that street. After Mom and Dad dropped me off, I would walk the half block to her house. While I took a lesson, they would drive to the church to take care of business.

Just before her house, I had to pass a house with a closed-in porch. In the dark winter evenings, I had a tremendous fear that someone would grab me from that porch and accost me. That fear did not help to build a love for those piano lessons.

That teacher used what I call an old-fashioned approach to instruction. She assigned three or four selections for me to practice one hour daily and expected me to perform them perfectly the next session. If I failed to master them to her satisfaction, I would have to repeat the ordeal week after week until they were done fluently. What she did not do was educate me on how to play the assigned numbers during the half hour under her tutelage!

At home, all I would do was sit at the piano and boringly wish the time away. When the hour was expired, I would breathe a sigh of relief, though musically my skills were not improved. My mind was tortured from week to week and my body from rear to tear.

For some, that might have been an excellent approach, but for a learner like me, it did not work. I was required to practice those selections daily even if I had problems understanding the content.

My cousin Betty recalled how I would literally hate to deal with the eighty-eight-key monster that sat in the teacher's studio and the one at home.

At every session, she acted as God and would strike my fingers with her saintly ruler if I unfortunately made errors. This was her way of encouraging me to do better and give me a complete love for those ivory keys as I labored in her prison of mortality-but what it did was create fear. She impressed upon me that at every session I should have the assigned selections mastered with no mistakes or else, especially if I practiced her required hours. I had to endure her method for four years! I have often wondered how many youngsters had or still have to endure that kind of treatment.

In today's society, with lawsuits cropping up due to abolished corporal punishment, specifically in the public schools, that kind of treatment would be challenged. One might ask the logical question, "Why did I not inform someone about her 'mighty' punishment for error?" I believed it was normal, and to an eight-year-old, revealing her severity to my parents, I imagined, would only make things worse; I feared their board of retribution. I, therefore, endured that kind of abuse as the lesser of two evils.

To add insult to injury, I had to perform polished selections every year in a recital. A youngster during one of the recitals was so petrified that an accident occurred while he was sitting on the bench. Fortunately, I escaped such an embarrassment, though having to play in public withered rather than built up my confidence. My hands would even freeze in that warm church auditorium. Nerves can do astounding things to one's psyche.

Needless to say, I did not master that instrument in four years. Because of her belief that I had no musical aptitude, she approached my parents and gave them the prediction that I would *never* master the piano and recommended that I be relieved of that responsibility.

How upset I became to realize that her ruler of inspiration would no longer strike my fingers! The withdrawal from those hours of daily practice saddened my ruptured ego. Actually, to me it was an escape to freedom.

Piano Lessons in Agony

Piano lessons for me were a chore.
In fact, I thought they were a complete bore.
Daily, I sat at the keys for an hour,
But those notes I had trouble to devour.

The teacher I had was a bit witty,
Striking my fingers, which was a pity.
When I bungled notes in a measure,
She would impede with haughty pleasure.

There are those who had to suffer like me,
Who could care less about a piano key.
They had instructors who were obtuse
Which, for them, caused much pain and abuse.

During those youth years, I was immature,
But she wanted me to play an overture.
I convinced myself I was sorely dumb,
Knowing an artist I would never become.

Oh, how wrong that idea became
As the thought of failure touched my brain.
I began to hear others who could play,
Wishing I would do the same someday.

Even though the teacher caused me to quit
And in fact thought of me as a misfit,
My parents did not give up on me,
Hoping failure was not my guarantee.

In college, I started to play for fun,
Abruptly wishing to perform for everyone.
There were professors who encouraged me
To become the best player I could be.

Let all who think they are no good
Look at life and be understood.
I was told a musician I'd never be
But scores have enjoyed my songs in this country.

In fifth grade, I continued to encounter devastation to my mental being. I had a difficult time solving reading problems in mathematics. Oh, I learned to add, subtract, multiply, and divide, but to work out the more complicated problems brought me fear.

I did not have dad's innate skill for solving those kinds of problems. He knew I had difficulty, and chose to come to my rescue by doing that work for me. I would then copy his accomplished work for the teacher to grade the next day.

Perhaps the teacher suspected that the skilled solutions came from a more sophisticated source. Why would she suddenly alter her routine?

One day, I was met head-on with a surprise! Instead of giving us the assignment to do at home, she had us do it at our desks. My blood pressure elevated as I helplessly sat there and did nothing. When the papers were collected, I was in deep trouble! She punished me by having me stay after school. What she should have done was investigate why I did not or could not do the assignment, and perhaps work with me until comprehension was accomplished.

I was too ashamed to tell her of my predicament. In that day, if one did not do his work, the problem was assumed to be indifference.

I also believe a wise decision on her part would have been to send each student to the chalkboard, and work through a problem, until it was understood. Perhaps with that approach, I would not have been in that dilemma. With a little patience, my dad should have worked with me the same way.

In mathematics, she used a method of teaching multiplication, that I have since appreciated. For twenty-five consecutive school days, the class had to write the times table from two through twelve. If one mistake occurred, the student would have to endure twenty-five more days, until perfection occurred. The student who sat behind me missed on the twenty-fourth day. I do believe after forty-nine days, he mastered it!

During that year, there were two embarrassing incidents that transpired. One day, I took a small bell to school that I decided to ring, while I ran around the building numerous times. One of the teachers became annoyed at the noise, and relieved me of its ownership. I often wondered what she did with it, because I never saw it again.

On another occasion, I became hungry while I was in class, and the hunger pangs became too much to bear. Luckily, I had an apple in my pocket. Lowering my head behind the student in front of me, I began to munch that fruit. Much to my chagrin, the teacher heard the munching. In front of the class, I was ordered to throw what was left of it into the wastebasket. Upon her desk rested a Ping-Pong paddle, which she used upon my seat of understanding. That day I learned a nutrition lesson—never eat in her class!

At the conclusion of the fifth grade, I received the worst news. My report card revealed, that I had failed three courses. Logic told me, that I should have been retained, but for some miraculous reason, an ultimatum was given to me. During the first grading period of grade six, if I received one failing grade, I would have to return to the fifth grade.

Shockingly, at the conclusion of the first grading period, I had three failing grades, but that dear teacher had a real concern and did not follow through with the threat (or perhaps she was unaware of the ultimatum). How embarrassing it would have been, had I been sent back to the fifth grade!

I took a liking to her style of teaching, and things began to improve. In fact, I was promoted without any blight on my record. Thank the Lord that she was a teacher who bolstered my devastated ego. I was fortunate to have her influence in my life, because she died a year later. I wonder what my situation would have been had another teacher been in charge.

With hindsight, I know why I was not demoted. Had that been my plight, my whole life would not have gone as it did. It was God's guiding hand!

Those years of piano lessons came to a screeching halt, while I was in the sixth grade, but Mom and Dad did not give up on me, providing me the opportunity to take accordion lessons. For six months, I struggled with that squeezebox. Again, it was not one of my fortes.

CHAPTER 3

Adolescence

During the outset of seventh grade, I became interested in playing the cornet, which is a little shorter than the trumpet. I asked my parents if I could take cornet lessons. Not only did they not adamantly say no, since I was a complete failure with the piano and accordion experiences, but they even bought me a new one.

For one year, I took lessons from an instructor who smoked cigarettes. I endured the foul air, because I began to enjoy that instrument.

In tenth grade, I joined the high school band, where each section of instrumentalists was seated by individual skills. The first-chair player was the most proficient. The cornet section had twelve members, and as I was initially placed in chair twelve, it behooved me to work hard to progress to chair one. During those three years, unfortunately, there were three others whom I could not dethrone.

Throughout those years, the band had concerts at our school and marched in parades. In Fredericksburg, Pennsylvania, the week of one Thanksgiving, our band marched in the town's annual parade. The weather became so bitterly cold that I had to hold my mouthpiece in my closed hand to keep it warm between musical selections.

In Palmyra, the band marched in an annual May Day parade. The temperature reached one hundred degrees, and it was so hot and humid that some parade members fainted.

As I improved, I was fortunate to accompany the congregational singing and play solos during the church services. While I was playing "Silent Night" on one occasion, I failed to reach the high note in the phrase "sleep in heavenly peace." Even though I was embarrassed, I learned early in life that one does not flee from opportunities because of errors.

An adult once told me never to turn down an opportunity, whether for musical renditions or public speaking. If I did, I might never have the opportunity again. How thankful I am that I heeded his advice!

In the spring of 1952, I was hired part-time at a roadside restaurant, where I prepared hamburgers, sliced potatoes for French fries, and scooped ice cream for sundaes and banana splits. To arrive there, I rode my father's motorbike. I parked it just outside the rear entrance. While on the job one evening, I glanced out the back door and saw that it had fallen on its side. I became concerned, since that was my transportation home at midnight. Not using common sense, I headed out the door and cranked up that motor to determine if it were still operable.

My employer spotted me and gave me the heave-ho. Perhaps I should have first voiced my concern about the problem and asked for permission to rev it up.

I was devastated, but that event was the beginning of the molding of the future of my entire life. It is thrilling how God could use that fallen motorbike and firing to change my life for His glory.

The restaurant building where I worked on Route 422

25

On June 9 of that spring, Mom and Dad took me to the Lebanon High School Auditorium, where the gospel film *Oil Town USA*, produced by the Billy Graham Association, was being shown. Because it has been more than fifty years since that day, I cannot remember the content of the film. The thrust at the conclusion, though, was for those who were not sure of eternity and heaven to accept Jesus Christ as their Savior. I became convicted that I was a sinner, asked Him to come into my heart, accepted Him as my own personal Savior, and became immediately born again. No longer was I headed to hell; I was assured of an eternal heaven, and a tremendous burden was lifted.

My whole outlook on life was transformed. A number of Scripture verses became real to me. The first was John 20:31 (KJV): "But these are written that ye might believe that Jesus is the Christ the Son of God, and that believing ye might have life through His name." Another was Romans 10:9-13 (KJV): "That if thou shalt confess with thy mouth the Lord Jesus and believe in thine heart that God hath raised him from the dead, thou shalt be saved. For with the heart man believeth unto righteousness and with the mouth confession is made unto salvation. For the scripture saith, whosoever believeth on him shall not be ashamed. For there is no difference between the Jew and the Greek: for the same Lord over all is rich unto all that call upon him. For whosoever shall call upon the name of the Lord shall be saved."

How could I not include perhaps the best-known verse, John 3:16 (KJV): "For God so loved the world, that he gave his only begotten Son, that whosoever believeth in him should not perish, but have everlasting life."

From God's Word, I learned that I could walk this life with total assurance of eternity in heaven with Jesus Christ. That assurance is specifically stated in 1 John 5:13 (KJV): "These things have I written unto you that believe on the name of the Son of God; that *ye may know* that ye have eternal life, and that ye may believe on the name of the Son of God."

Before June 9, I had told individuals that I was saved and was even baptized, but I could not remember a time when I asked Christ to come into my life. I had complete insecurity about what would happen if I died. Thinking that I would be embarrassed, if I revealed the decision

I had made, I kept what I did quiet. There was a joy that transpired, though, and I could not remain silent for long.

About two days later, I sheepishly asked my mother how a person can be sure of heaven and what one must do to get there when he dies. I really asked her, trusting that she would give me an answer that would fortify my belief that what I had done was correct. I respected her knowledge of Scripture, and wanted the answer she gave to me to affirm, that what I did was in agreement with God's Word.

Her answer was based upon John 3:3 (KJV), which says, "Except a man be born again he cannot see the kingdom of God."

Proudly, I told her the news, that I trusted Christ in the Lebanon High School Auditorium. At first, I anticipated a negative response, such as, "You said in the past that you were saved. Are you confused?" She immediately said that I did exactly what the Bible says to do, and rejoiced that I had made sure of my salvation, and shared the news to her first. Before then, in church and elsewhere, I professed Christ, but never really confessed Christ. There is a 100 percent difference, which is proven in Romans 10:9-13 (KJV).

A number of years later, I heard a message about the importance of following the Lord in baptism, once one is born again. I began to squirm in my seat realizing that I had the cart before the horse. I shared with my pastor, that I was baptized earlier, when I was not saved, and as a true believer, I needed to be baptized again. With that he agreed, and I had the privilege to tell the congregation my testimony, and was baptized as God intended it.

Not long after my conversion day, I had the jubilant occasion to lead a neighbor friend of mine to Christ in our kitchen. That experience was just as gratifying as my acceptance of Christ!

A few weeks later, a woman, who was a member of my church, approached me to invite me to work at Mt. Lou San Bible Camp, which is located six miles east of Harrisburg, along the foothills of the Appalachian Mountains. She said I would be paid five dollars a week to be the dishwasher. Had I not been fired from that roadside job, I would have had to decline, but I cheerfully accepted the opportunity. Money to a fifteen year-old was not an issue. Going to camp was! That decision was crucial, since I needed much spiritual guidance.

Think of it, she could have asked any of the young people from our church to fill that sole position, and they could have said yes, but that opportunity, I believe, was the Lord's will and the laying of the foundation to my future.

At the beginning of July, I packed my suitcases, and was camp bound with my cornet, leaving the comfort of home for eight weeks.

Because it was a Bible camp, there was a gospel meeting every day in the chapel. The director of the camp, a dedicated man of God, would share his faith, and biblically teach the Word of God to the campers. The purpose of his exhortation was to win those who were lost to Christ, ground them in the faith, and trust that they would leave at the end of their stay with a committed desire to read the Bible, pray daily, grow spiritually, and share the greatest message with a lost and dying world.

During one of the services, there was a thrust for those who trusted Christ to take the next step and dedicate their lives to the Lord. That evening, in my room, which was located in the rear of the tabernacle, I took that next step, and dedicated my life to Him. At my bedside, I said to the Lord, "Lord, take my life, my cornet, and everything to be used for Thy glory from this day forth." Dedication is different from being born again. Being born again is the first step. Dedication is the next step. Nahum 1:7 (KJV) became my life's verse: "The Lord is good, a stronghold in the day of trouble; and he knoweth them that trust in him."

Since I took my cornet to the camp, one day I suggested the idea to the director that I stand outside the circle of twelve cabins, and play a gospel hymn and reveille to wake up the campers in the morning, and a hymn and taps at the close of the day. He thought the idea was unique, better than the sound of a bell, and told me to do it. That began to alleviate my fear of playing in public, and needless to say, the compliments from the campers and staff started to build up my self-esteem.

During the chapel services, there was a need for a pianist. Four years had passed, since I had taken lessons. I knew I was not skilled enough to play for them, and I was not about to step up to that piano and attempt to play.

A deep desire began to stir within me to learn, as I envisioned myself playing for the services.

There were two pianos at the camp, where I was able to strike the keys for the first time. Since I was told I would never learn to play, it would have been a thrill for me to play for the services, but I was no longer able to play with both hands at the same time.

I borrowed a camp hymnbook, studied the notes of simple hymns, played one hand at a time, and a second experience at those keyboards began.

On Saturdays, it was thrilling to hike the one-thousand-foot mountain with the campers. At the top, we approached the over two-thousand-mile Appalachian Trail, which is a meandering path on the crest of the mountains from Maine to Georgia. From that height, there were treeless areas, where I could gander at the scene for miles. It was a dream world come true: the view, the smell of pine trees, the fresh air, and the wonder of God's magnificent creation.

On that mountain, we had to be alert in the event that we encountered snakes, especially rattlesnakes. I saw a number of blacksnakes, but we were told they were harmless.

On one of those hikes, we decided to take a shortcut, and trudge across a farmer's pasture, that was located halfway up the mountain. Trees surrounded the fenced-in pasture. What was not in our vision, was a herd of bulls in the distance! Once we spotted them, we were too far into the pasture to retreat. Horribly, they began to bolt in our direction, and we bolted in return! How lucky we were, that no one stumbled or was trampled! We escaped by climbing over the fence just in the nick of time.

That eight-week summer dishwashing job in the sizzling-hot temperatures was totally agonizing torture for a fifteen-year-old, but the other activities help me endure. To climb that mountain, beat off the bugs, build fireplaces, enjoy the fresh air, enjoy the benefit of the physical exercise, aid the director and assistant directors, and receive the spiritual blessings from God's Word, changed my life.

The next summer, I again worked at that camp, but this time, only as a helper doing outdoor chores with the assistant director. What fun that was, as I picked up debris, hiked that mountain, did other odds and ends, continued to play the cornet, dabbled again at playing the piano, and prepared the outdoor fireplaces for the Saturday wiener roasts and bonfires! At the bonfire services, gospel songs were sung, testimonials from campers, who were saved or had grown in the faith were shared, and the devotionals from Scripture were inspiring.

There were some things of nature that I'll never forget. That is the only place, where I have seen pawpaw bushes. A fruit from the bushes ripens in the fall and tastes similar to cantaloupe. I loved to smell the tea with a small leaf that permeated the area with the odor of mint. In the creek that flows at the foot of the mountain and the border of the camp, I also had fun catching crawfish and turtles.

The camp is only about twenty miles west of the former Fort Indiantown Gap Army military training ground. If the wind blew from the east, the rumbling sound of cannons used in training could easily be heard being fired.

As I said, the two summers that I spent at the camp were a growth period spiritually for me, but I had another blessed experience. One fall, I spent a weekend retreat with another Bible-believing group. The highlight was the hike we took to the top of the mountain following the Appalachian Trail about three miles toward the Susquehanna River. At that point there was a clearing, where future power lines would exist. We stopped there, sat upon rocks, and had an inspiring devotion by the leader, praising God for His goodness, and the promise of eternal life for those who were saved.

He made a statement that I have not forgotten. "As we congregate here today to praise the Lord, remember that this is the only time, that this total group will gather together again on this side of heaven. If all of us have trusted Jesus Christ as our Savior, we will meet again in heaven." What a heartrending and comforting truth that that message was to me!

The neighborhood where I grew up was isolated from the hustle and bustle of Lebanon, with its population of approximately thirty-three thousand. Our four or five blocks were located near farmers' fields where corn, tomatoes, potatoes, wheat, and alfalfa were grown.

Even though there were not many youth, we certainly found enough activities to do. For instance, after the wheat or alfalfa was cut and baled, the gang used one field as a baseball diamond. Blocks of wood or rocks were used for the bases.

With a little ingenuity, I was able to create a basketball court next to our house. Two trees were located a good distance apart, and I nailed backstops and anchored hoops to them. I spread ashes from the furnace that were excellent for the floor once the rain made them solid. We spent hours at a time playing games or just shooting the basketball.

Once a month, the neighborhood gang boarded a school bus, and spent the evening at the roller rink in Mount Gretna, located in a small mountain range three miles south of Lebanon. One of those months, a friend of mine, who had his driver's license, took me to the rink. After an enjoyable evening, while we were heading home, a policeman was nearing us with his red lights flashing. My friend thought he had broken the law, and pressed his foot on the gas pedal. Thinking he could outrun the trooper, he made a quick left turn onto a side road, turned off his headlights, and within a few yards ran into the gutter. He could have killed us both. The amazing thing about the ordeal was that the policeman was after another driver!

The YMCA in Lebanon had swimming classes. After I completed the six sessions, I failed to learn, because of the fear I had of water.

When I did learn, it was not with an instructor, and the method was not advisable. On a farmer's property, there was a dam that was fed by a creek. At the mouth of the dam, the creek had a width of about fifteen feet. Crudely, I gesticulated and made it from one side to the other. The water was deeper than six feet.

That dam

Lights Dam, which is now called Lion's Lake, is adjacent to where Mom grew up. It is about a quarter mile in length and very deep. In time, my fear of water dissipated, and I began to swim the length with no supervision. I should have given thought to the risk of becoming tangled in the seaweed, that grew very thick in many areas, or of developing a cramp at any time, crippling any possibility of my making it to shore or being rescued.

Light's Dam

About three-quarters of a mile to the east of our former home is a limestone quarry. Some of us brave ones would sneak to the bottom, where there was deep freshwater, swim approximately one hundred feet from one side to the other, climb the steep bank, and leap or dive from the protruding rocks thirty or forty feet above the water. All this was also done on forbidden territory, and without lifeguards or life-saving equipment.

There was a young man in our neighborhood that was as foolish as we were in another quarry in the Lebanon area. In the darkness of the night, he went with his buddies, and began to jump off of the cliffs. He misjudged his aim, hit a rock, and lost his life.

We did not always swim in dangerous places. There was a huge public swimming pool near the border of Lebanon. One summer day, a neighbor friend and I rode our bicycles the three or four miles to the pool to cool off. Our fun was cut short that afternoon when a dangerous thunderstorm developed, forcing the swimmers to leave the pool. I wisely moved into a nearby building where pop and candy were sold. My friend unwisely dashed under a tree moments before lightning struck one of the limbs, which crashed to the ground, exactly where she had been standing. In the nick of time, she bolted to the building, and escaped injury or death.

To the north of Avon Heights were sections of the Union Canal, which is the oldest canal in the United States. For a number of years, it was used to transport goods to and from the Schuylkill River in Reading and the Susquehanna River in Harrisburg. North of Lebanon is another preserved section of the canal, where the oldest tunnel in the United States is located.

During the winter, there were still parts of the canal, where the ice was wide and thick enough to play ice hockey. For a puck, we used an empty tin can, and for hockey sticks, limbs from trees sufficed. The fact that we survived and escaped being bitten by the huge rats that lived on the banks or breaking any bones had to be miraculous, because we played with reckless abandon and without protective garb.

My aunt lived two or three feet from the edge of the steep bank above the canal. One winter day, when the temperature rose above thirty-two degrees, I informed her that my neighbor and I had planned to walk on the ice. She warned us not to go, because it might have become thin. We did not heed her advice and crazily took a chance. Without warning, the ice shattered, and my neighbor received a wet, bone-chilling experience. How fortunate it was, that the water was no more than three feet deep! She worked her way to safety soaked and shivering. Think of the consequence for our disobedience had the water been much deeper! I was far enough away from her, that I was spared the freezing, wet plunge!

The Union Canal and oldest tunnel in the United States in Lebanon,
three miles from where we ice-skated and played hockey

The sign

On a somewhat warm day, another friend and I made a thoughtless decision and ignorantly stepped on the ice of a water-filled mine hole about a mile to the south of our home. We stayed near the edge, and without warning we heard a crack. The ice shattered under my friend's feet but again not mine. Instinctively, he grabbed a low-hanging limb that was thick enough to hold his weight and just above the broken ice, sparing his life! How close we came to slipping into eternity!

We learned after that experience to chop a hole into the ice, to determine if the thickness were no more than three inches, and to stay off, if the temperature rose higher than thirty-two degrees. When it rises above freezing, ice does not melt evenly.

That mine hole and me

One summer day that friend and I hiked from one farmer's field to another. Along a fence, that divided the two fields, we spotted an animal hole near the foot of a tree stump. We gathered some dead grass and shoved it into the hole. Hoping we could smoke out an animal, we set the grass on fire with matches I had in my pocket. The fire spread to the tree stump and then farther. Helplessly, we dashed from the scene, as our plan went up in smoke. We did not stop to consider what would have been our plight had we been burned, had acres of land been burned, or had a vicious animal been smoked out of its domain.

There was a very steep, and tremendously high hill, where the neighborhood gang could sled ride for hours, even in the moonlight. Just to arrive at the top was impossible without using the pointed runners of the back of our sleds to give us the boost to make it to the crest.

My buddy and I decided to challenge the dangerous bumps of the slope by riding double on my sled. While we gained speed, and bounced wickedly toward the bottom, the wind wet our eyes with tears causing us to lose our sense of direction. Strangely, the ride became totally smooth. We did not realize that we had become airborne, flying perhaps more than twenty feet, and landed in the middle of the nearby asphalt road. When we hit the road, our weight and impact smashed my sled in two. Miraculously, we had perfect balance, while we were gliding. Fortunately, no automobile met us at the point of impact.

Of course, we were not satisfied that we could have smashed our bones or lost our lives. Up to the top of that hill we trudged again, made an immediate decision to ride double on his sled, and on the way down the hill, smashed his sled in two.

The hill as it is today.
Tons of dirt were removed years ago.

In the fall, my buddy and I thought we would be intelligent, took weed sprigs into the backyard shed, and struck a match to the ends to smoke them like cigarettes. Just after they started to burn, we heard the back door of my house slam. Dad must have suspected we were up to no good, and caught us red-handed. He ordered me to go into our house and my buddy to his home.

I expected his wrath to come down on me. Perhaps that never occurred because before he accepted Christ, he was a smoker, and knew that I would be faced with the same temptation.

So grateful I am that he came on the scene when he did, because we did not have time to smoke the weeds. Smoking them, I learned later, would have been worse than smoking cigarettes. Since that day, I have never had the desire to put one cigarette to my lips. Health-wise and as a testimony for Jesus Christ, I am thankful, that I never started that addictive habit!

That buddy practically defeated me in every activity. At nearby ponds, he would catch more fish. When we played board games, he won. On the side-yard basketball court, he scored more points. In school, he was in the same classes and always scored higher.

Because he was in the same classes as I was, he was also in my typing class. Every day we had speed drills, and the five fastest students' names were printed on the chalkboard with the fastest one appearing first. I felt like a king, since my name usually was number one. In that class, I beat him in every drill. I really needed that to build up my self-esteem.

I appreciated the variety of activities we did as a family. For instance, Norman and I enjoyed hunting with our dad. Once the farmers finished harvesting the crops, and the hunting season began in November, they toted the shotguns. I had a fear of guns, but I still enjoyed trudging through the fields with them. For successful results, we took our beagle. Once he picked up the scent of the game, he would begin to run and howl, which was the signal to be ready to shoot, because he was in pursuit of either a rabbit or a pheasant.

Many times, Mom and Dad took us fishing to various places, such as the Susquehanna River near Harrisburg and a number of small dams. Once I felt the tug of a hooked fish and actually caught one, I became hooked!

They also managed to give my brother and me the opportunity to see distant places to help us appreciate some of God's creation. One of those trips was to Niagara Falls and the surrounding attractions. There we viewed the falls with their continuous mist, rode an elevator that lowered us behind the falls, and experienced the thunderous sound, took a ride in the dangling cable car over the swirling Niagara River, saw the gigantic outdoor clock surrounded by colorful flowers, and stood at the lock, that raises and lowers the ships from Lake Erie and the Saint Lawrence River!

On some Sundays, after morning church and dinner, they would take us on long drives. Since the foot of the Appalachian Mountains is only ten miles from where we lived, we would often head there, and see the beauty of the mountains-and catch panoramic views of the unsightly-stripped coalmines. Coal was, or perhaps still is, retrieved with steam shovels digging deep into the surface of those scenic Pennsylvania Mountains, leaving unsightly quarries. Strip mines differ from underground mines. Underground mines have an entrance, where railroad tracks are placed and used by miners to descend deep into the earth, where the coal is dynamited loose and brought to the surface in railcars.

On other Sundays, we traveled about twenty-eight miles to Harrisburg, headed north a number of miles, turned east between the first two mountain ranges, and drove until we arrived near the Indiantown Gap army training grounds.

Once we traveled between those mountains and followed a horrendous thunderstorm. Thankfully, we were on the tail end, because it produced hailstones the size of baseballs that crushed automobile windows and smashed home and industrial roofs. In amazement, Dad stopped our car and picked up a few. We were so impressed, that we photographed and kept them in our freezer for months, until they totally evaporated.

In those mountains, was a spring, where we would fill bottles with fresh water. Not far from that sight, we found an abundance of blueberries. Carefully, I sat on a rock near the top of a steep bank to retrieve some of those berries, unaware that underneath that rock, there was a yellow jacket nest. Within seconds, I was swarmed and stung repeatedly. Desperately, I dashed to our automobile and escaped more of their wrath.

The Yellow Jacket Attack

One day when I was a child,
My parents took me into the wild.
Into our car they put a big pan.
To pick blueberries was their plan.

I was so excited when we arrived,
That my hunger pangs were revived.
For the entire day, we picked and ate
Those juicy berries until it was late.

While I was looking down a steep gully,
I found some to put into my belly.
To retrieve them, I sat on a rock,
But what I received was a stinging shock.

A yellow jacket nest was located, where I sat.
They stung me all over-just like that.
My good parents, knew I was afraid,
And rapidly gave me first aid.

During the summer of 1953, we took a vacation in our brand-new Buick to Wyoming. At that time, there were very few interstate highways that enabled us to travel through small towns, and really enjoy the view of the country. One town had a sign that read Population 6. That had to be the smallest town in America.

Astonished, I was at the contrast of scenery, as we traveled from east of the Mississippi River and throughout the western states. East of the river, there are forests, tree-laden mountains, hills, and farmers' fields. There were miles of cornfields closer to the west bank of the river, but the farther west that we traveled the scenery became more and more different. The land was absolutely flat and barren with straight roads for hundreds of miles.

The next stops on our trip were Mount Rushmore and the Badlands of South Dakota. The meandering snake-like road that led to that tourist attraction caused Norman to become violently ill. In spite of having nothing to ease Norman's illness, Dad decided to continue the trip westward with his objective of reaching the coast of California.

One who has never ridden over the Bighorn Mountains in Wyoming needs that experience to appreciate America's beauty at its best! The drive to the top with nothing blocking one's view is absolutely breathtaking, especially from twenty thousand feet above sea level. Some sections of that road were next to chasms of thousands of feet with no guardrails. Fearfully, I just knew that Dad would lose control. How happy I was, when we reached the bottom of the western side!

After some eighty miles more of flat land and straight roads, we stopped in Cody, Wyoming, where we enjoyed a rodeo, and spent the night in a motel with a magnificent view of the next range of the Rocky Mountains just to the west.

The next day we continued our trip up that mountain to the Yellowstone National Park. Roaming the road and forest of Yellowstone were herds of moose, buffalo, bears, and other animals. One bear appeared to be very friendly. Dad had a cracker, and decided to share it with the hungry beast. For his kindness, Norman, who took the picture, was bitten and slightly injured. Wisely, he fed no more food to nature's furry animals.

That hungry bear

As we drove around the park, we smelled the nauseous rotten-egg odor of numerous geysers. That drive would not have been complete without stopping at the famous geyser, Old Faithful, which erupts with steam once every hour.

In contrast, the smell of pine trees permeated the air, especially at the cabin, where we stayed for the night. The owners had horses and charged one dollar to ride on a trail about fifty feet above an absolutely gorgeous lake in front of the snow-capped Grand Teton Mountains. The trail was close enough to the edge, that one slip of the horse could have been tragic. What an exhilarating experience for a sixteen-year-old!

Me on the horse

At the cabins, a squirrel was sitting upon a young lady's arm drinking Coke from the bottle, while it was being held. Who would ever believe, that a wild squirrel could become friendly enough to sit upon this woman's wrist and drink pop? I wonder how long it took her to train that wild animal.

The amazing Coke-drinking squirrel

We really wanted to see California and the Pacific coast, but Norman's condition worsened, thus preventing our traveling farther west.

The next morning, we started our trip down the mountain. As Dad applied the brakes, he helplessly discovered that they were not engaging. The descent was horrifying as our new car swerved around dangerous curves. Thankfully, we made it down one of the steepest mountains in the United States. We had no choice, but to continue about two hundred miles without brakes across the wilderness, seeing few automobiles, numerous killed jackrabbits, and sagebrush. That we drove without an accident all the way to a repair shop in Denver was shocking!

We were not able to find medicine for Norman, until we stayed at a motel in West Virginia. A drug store near there had the needed medicine, and his condition improved.

That trip would not have been complete without our seeing the Endless Caverns in the Shenandoah Valley of Virginia. I am thankful that Dad and Mom took us into a place under the earth with its stalagmites and stalactites that perhaps most will never see.

Another family activity, that we did once every summer was to board a trolley that traveled fifteen miles in the center of Route 422 from Lebanon to Hershey Park, which opened daily at 1:00 p.m. It seemed like an eternity passed, before the moment we arrived at the amusement park. I could tell when we were approaching Hershey, because of the aroma of the chocolate factory adjacent to the park.

In the forties and fifties, the park was more family-oriented. There were picnic areas, where we brought our baskets of food, and safely left them until lunchtime.

One bought tickets to board the rides. Kids' rides were ten cents, and rides for teenagers and adults were twenty-five cents. We would enjoy them, until our money was depleted. Today, one pays a set price to enter the park, and can enjoy the activities all day.

Perhaps, because of the popularity and financial success of other amusement parks throughout the years, Hershey did a major facelift, modernizing nearly everything. The original roller coaster with the ninety-foot hill is still there.

Destroyed were the funhouse with Laughing Sal, an old-lady-mannequin, that was bent over laughing incessantly, and could be heard outside of the building; the laugh-land building with various activities, such as a huge horizontal moving wooden barrel, which one hoped not to fall, while balancing from one end to the other, vertically curved mirrors, that distorted the image of one's body; and holes in the floor, that an inconspicuous person controlled with a button, when pushed would force air upward and lift women's dresses.

Electrically controlled cars were in another facility, allowing the driver to crash into other moving vehicles with the desire to create a jam.

The mill shoot had boats that followed moving water. Just before the end of the ride was a steep hill. From the top, the boat took a steep plunge, and all on board were guaranteed to be soaked.

The pretzel ride followed a track in the dark, and unexpected objects would appear to scare those on board.

I can still envision the outside band stage with the wooden benches for daily concerts. "Saber Dance" and "Seventy-Six Trombones" left an impression on me.

The park etched such memories in me, that I wrote a song called "Hershey Park," which was sung by the 150-member John Marshall High School choir in Cleveland, Ohio, before the entire student body, and at the annual concert for parents in 2001.

Page one of "Hershey Park" song
Areas of Hershey Park today

Photo 1: The park sign

Photo 2: The original chocolate factory as seen from the
kissing tower and the Hershey Park monorail

Photo 3: The train

Photo 4: A water ride

Photo 5: Roller coasters

Photo 6: The hotel

Physical problems developed, when acne covered my face, causing a fear, that I would be marred for life. To add insult to injury, about every two weeks, an agonizing sty would nearly close my eyes with swelling. Because of those conditions, there were those in my classes at school that would mock me. I felt like crawling into seclusion and never appearing in public. If those who harassed me had to endure the physical pain and embarrassment that I experienced, perhaps there would have been empathy for my condition instead. In addition to their mocking, looking into mirrors made me feel even more debased and ugly.

My concerned mother made an appointment for me to see a dermatologist. After months of medical procedures, my face problem improved, and I was left with no physical scars.

Since I had received Christ as my Savior, even with the problems of insecurity in a number of areas of my life-the belief that I was not very intelligent, the frustration of studying, and the mental scars left by my face problem-my outlook on life slowly changed for the better and my academic-standing improved.

During my senior year, our class was fortunate to take a three-day trip to Washington, DC, and visit many government buildings such as the Capitol, the White House, and the Washington Monument. We completely defrayed the expenses by having a contest for two weeks to sell household products. I really had the craving to win, because the winner would receive a new watch. Because I sold products to many people, I believed I would win. I kept very secretive about how well I was doing and overwhelmingly won.

Through the grapevine, I heard that my buddy was also doing very well and thought he would easily win. When he learned that I won, he ostracized me for about nine months. He was a believer in Christ, admitted he was wrong, apologized, and said that I deserved the watch more than he did. Our friendship was restored.

The trip started with a negative. While we were heading to Washington on the chartered bus, a young man in the seat in front of me decided to test my faith by lighting a cigar and blowing the smoke into my face the entire trip. Instead of making an issue of it, which the driver or chaperones should have done, I did nothing to contest his nasty behavior. I do not know, if I shared my faith with him, but I could have.

Perhaps that is why, he attempted to see, if I would fall from grace by using inappropriate language in retaliation.

On the very first night, while I was in the sixth-floor hotel room, my three roommates decided stupidly to cast water balloons out of the open window and struck pedestrians on the sidewalk below. Since they heaved them out of the sixth-floor window, and it was after sunset, they assumed they would not be caught. The angered management and the police dashed into our room and rushed us to the first floor, where we were all charged with disorderly conduct. At that moment, one of the roommates, who was a friend of mine, said, "Fox is innocent." Because of his statement, I was excused. They could have been forced to spend the night on a bus ride back to Lebanon, but they were fortunate to receive a warning.

Senior Trip

While I was a student in the twelfth grade,
My high school class travelled to Washington.
Everyone who took that excursion
Was supposed to act normal and have fun.

To travel to our destination,
We boarded a swanky Greyhound bus.
Before we left on that long journey,
We were told not to muss or even cuss.

As we headed down that long highway,
Not everyone listened to that advice.
Since I was a born-again Christian,
I knew it was important for me to act nice.

A simple-minded classmate thought he was funny
And lit a cigar, blowing smoke in my face.
He wanted to test my righteous patience,
Hoping I would fall out of God's grace.

At the hotel, four of us gentlemen
Stayed in the same room for more than one night.
From high above the pavement below,
Some threw water balloons from the sixth-floor height.

Before long, the director came to our room
And demanded that we dash to the first floor.
There we were greeted by the policemen
While we waited near the office door.

As I stood, worried that I would be charged,
I did not have to make any comment,
Since one of my friends came to my defense,
Stating I was completely innocent.

Those who played that game of ignorance
Could have found their vacation cut short,
Escorted to the police station
And from their happy domain abort.

That week, I rejoiced that I had obeyed the law
By not following the whims of the gang,
Because, when we were corralled red-handed,
I was freed from the ordeal and sprang.

Senior class men
I am third from the left in first row.

MAY, 1954

Senior class women

That spring, I proudly walked across the South Lebanon High School auditorium stage, and received my hard-earned diploma. Next to our house, I stood wearing my graduation gown and tassel.

Freedom day

CHAPTER 4

After Graduation

Graduation from high school in May of 1954 was a big relief to me. After I moved that tassel from one side of my head to the other, and was congratulated by my proud parents and brother, I drove my 1941 Plymouth, which my parents had given to me, when I received my driver's license, to the graduation party. As I drove, I thought, "I am free—free of high school, homework, obligated reading, mathematics, science, and, of course, tests!" But how free was I? Little did I know how many tests still faced me—not only subject tests, but also the voluminous others, that would not fade in this life.

Quickly, I learned, that no one is ever free except in Christ. Even if one owns his own business, he is not free. It did not take very long for me to realize how free I'd become, after I held my diploma. Questions erupted in my mind, as I drove alone in that vehicle. What lay ahead for me? What kind of career I pursue? What college, if any, would accept a "flunky" like me? Even before I contacted any college, I was convinced, that no institution would believe I could handle college courses.

A counselor at Camp Mt. Lou San, who was a student in a Bible college in New York, recommended that I apply there. To be accepted, I had to take a college entrance exam to determine, if I were able to handle a college curriculum. Nervously, I agonized through that exam. Much to my dismay, I must have done very poorly, because I received a rejection letter from the admissions director, giving me the discouraging news, that he did not wish to take a chance on my coming there and not making the grade. Thank God that that rejection did not prove to be my downfall. Actually, it played in my favor; it proved to be God's direction for great experiences to follow.

Mom and Dad continued to have communication with our former pastor, who became the pastor of that Baptist church in Wellington, Ohio. They had a son, who was a student at Piedmont Bible College (now called Piedmont Baptist University as of 2012) in Winston-Salem, North Carolina. They contacted him about my plight. He wasted no time recommending me to that admission's director.

A few weeks later, I received an application that I immediately completed and returned. There was no pre-test to be taken—all I needed was patience, while I waited for a response.

In the meantime, I was hired to work on a farm. For a number of weeks, I organized heavy bales of hay six tiers high on the wagons. It was crucial, that they not crash to the ground, as the wagon bounced across bumpy fields.

July and August is harvest time for ripened wheat. I rode the wagon, and informed the farmer, when the burlap bags were full. To protect my lungs from the dust, I had to wear a nose mask. By the end of the day, I was sweaty and filthy black in the sweltering heat.

Throughout that summer, I also had two other employments. One was a plastic factory, where I was hired to do piece work. I was paid by how fast I could move one-eighth-inch-thin plastic on to a fast-rotating rod from left to right without any of the rod exposed. That coiled plastic was then used to produce women's purses.

During my third day on that job, a rod slipped off the machine used by one of the workers and rammed through his arm. The sight of his bloodied arm was all it took to convince me to quit instantly, before the same fate befell me.

For the other short-lived job, I picked peaches and cherries for a few dollars a day.

CHAPTER 5

After High School and the Next Challenge

In the middle of August, I received the shocking acceptance letter from Piedmont Bible College. That great news set in motion the important task of preparing immediately a list of the necessities for college life.

Reality suddenly struck me that I was about to be severed from my parents, after more than seventeen years. With a sense of skepticism and even fear, I was about to embark on a new avenue of life. I really began to wonder, if I could pass the courses. The earlier rejection from that New York Bible College helped to cause that fear. What would happen, if the opinion of that admissions director proved valid? How would I face my family, the members of my home church, and even my friends? I would have been totally embarrassed!

More thoughts entered my mind. What kind of roommates would I have? Would we get along? Would the lifestyle in the north be different from the one in Dixie? What kind of food would I have to eat? Would the professors be helpful, when I faced subject difficulties? Would the needed finances be supplied? Six hundred dollars for room, board, and tuition at that time was enormous. It was important for me to remember the Lord's promise as stated in Philippians 4:19 (KJV): "But my God shall supply all your need according to his riches in Glory by Christ Jesus."

A number of days, before I started the trip south in my old Plymouth, I informed my dad, that it seemed to have a mechanical problem. To check for himself, he test-drove it and determined, that the problem was in my head. He was convinced, but I was not.

In spite of my doubt, I reluctantly began the trip, trusting his opinion was correct. As I was driving on Route 29 through Virginia, and far from any city, my car sputtered and broke down next to a mechanic's garage. Some might call that a coincidence, but I know, it was the Lord's protection.

After analyzing the situation, the mechanic determined, that he would need at least two days for the problem to be fixed. Kindly, he allowed me to use his phone to call Mom and Dad long distance to inform them of my dilemma.

About five or six hours later, they found me, thanks to the directions given them by the mechanic.

My belongings were transferred to their car so we could proceed to the college, let the administration know about our problem, take my things to my dorm room, and stay at our former pastor's home at their kind invitation. They were no longer in Ohio, but were ministering in a church in the town of Draper, North Carolina.

Two days later, we drove back to the shop. The mechanic informed us, that the car was driven on one cylinder, which had less than 25 percent thrust. How I drove approximately two hundred miles with my car in that pitiful condition seemed unbelievable, but was actually miraculous! At that juncture Dad paid the bill and headed north with Mom, while I returned to the college.

After living under the protective wings of my parents, and being accepted by Piedmont, I was about to encounter different responsibilities and new experiences in life. I was about to meet men preparing for the ministry—men who had converged from other parts of the United States and the world with diverse personalities, ideas, and habits.

When I entered my dorm room that first day, I saw four bunks. What a surprise to learn, that I would have three roommates for the next few years! A rapid adjustment in my thinking had to be made, since they were from different backgrounds and neighborhoods-and of course with idiosyncrasies! To get along, we had to learn how important it was to be unselfish and have respect for one another.

The men's two-story dormitory was probably a converted old mansion. All of us had to share the same bathroom and shower facility.

That was inconvenient, when many from both floors had to ready themselves for classes at the same time.

My home was located in Pennsylvania Dutch country, which includes the Lebanon, Lancaster, and Reading areas. Many of the residents communicate in what is called Pennsylvania Dutch. In that region, the folks have a German accent. There was a young man on campus, who would bend over with uncontrolled laughter, whenever he heard me speak, because he was only accustomed to Southern drawl, and thought my accent was humorous. I could have taken offense, but I laughed with him. I believe, that it never occurred to him, that perhaps his accent was just as strange to me.

The first full week was class registration. After thoughtful consideration, I chose to enroll in the bachelor of theology degree program, which would take five years of concentrated study of the Word of God from Genesis to Revelation. That vein of study is for prospective pastors, pastors desiring more training, Sunday school teachers, or anyone wishing to know the Bible better, so he or she could effectively serve the Lord, wherever He leads. My life's direction was not yet determined, but I was ready for the challenge.

For one who registered as a full-time degree student, eighteen semester hours of class work had to be taken each half year. This involved assimilating information from professors, and having discussions in class eighteen hours per week for eighteen weeks, equaling five or more subjects. There was no time for frivolous living. I could not afford to get behind in any course!

As I entered the first week in that degree program, I needed to learn very quickly, what was essential. With the help of concerned roommates, friends, and professors giving me ideas on how to study, I began to comprehend the most important material quickly.

Within a few days, the reality struck me, that the amount of studying under pressure, the meeting of deadlines, the pressure of taking tests, and the fear of forgetting, what I did assimilate were very exhausting and nerve-racking.

During that first year, I might have come close to a nervous breakdown. While I was in the library, where silence was expected, one of my friends was sitting across the table from me and sneezed. I took one glance at him, as the sneeze erupted, and I began to laugh. The longer I laughed, the more hysterical I became. I even lost the knowledge, of why I was laughing. Those who were there realized I was in trouble, and escorted me out of the library. Fortunately, no emergency personnel were needed.

One of the first courses I took was Old Testament Survey, an overview of the Old Testament books of the King James Bible taught by Professor Herbert Brown. When he gave the first exam, many in the class, including me, failed. He did not wish for anyone to start college life as a failure, allowed further study of the same content, and gave us a second chance. Thankfully, I passed that test and the course.

Since I was preparing to be a minister of the gospel of Jesus Christ, I took a course called Comparative Religions that helped me to become more grounded in God's Word and specifically what is in contradiction to His Word. That course was essential because 1 Peter 3:15 (KJV) says, "But sanctify the Lord God in your hearts: and be ready always to give an answer to every man that asketh you a reason of the hope that is in you with meekness and fear: having a good conscience; that, whereas they speak evil of you, as of evildoers, they may be ashamed that falsely accuse your good conversation in Christ." It was not a simple task to separate the basics of so many religions, but by putting feet to my prayers and tedious studying, I managed!

As I continued to study God's Word, the Lord opened my eyes to a very important truth. No matter what differences there are between religions, I did not accept a religion, when I was born again. Also, when I shared my faith, I learned to stick to the message of the Bible, which gives the only way to heaven. It is *not what man thinks is correct, but what the Word of God says is the way!* In John 14:6 (KJV), Jesus said, "I am the way, the truth and the life: no man cometh unto the Father but by me."

I brought my cornet that first year, planning to practice whenever opportunities arose, but the thought of playing the piano did not escape my mind, and on occasions I would play. As the urge grew, I found a piano teacher, who taught me for a number of months.

Some weeks before Christmas vacation, I was hired part time at a department store not far from the college to assemble toys. One day, I glanced out the back window, because I heard an automobile accident.

That evening, while I was in the dorm, I heard another crash. I went outside and ran full speed along the dark path to view the crash, but ran nose first into a tree. I became the third accident in one day, and felt the agonizing pain.

Winston-Salem is the home of R. J. Reynolds Tobacco Company. We at Piedmont did not smoke, and even hated the noxious air, that was emitted from that factory, when the winds blew from the east. A number of us still decided to take a tour of the facility located about a mile from the campus.

Inside the main entrance, was a full-sized camel, which was constructed totally of shreds of tobacco leaves. Further into the plant were millions of cigarettes on a conveyer ready for inspection. Any that were not the appropriate length, or had any imperfections were discarded.

The tour was fascinating, but I have thought about the millions of people, who have contracted cancer, heart disease, putrefied the air, and burned their hard-earned wages as a consequence of smoking the billions of cigarettes produced yearly in that factory.

Though the road was difficult that first year, my dedication to the task paid off. I passed the courses, headed home for the summer with my head held high, and was ready for my sophomore year.

My parents helped me financially that first year, but I knew, that it was imperative for me to find a summer job to help defray the educational expenses for the next year. Since construction jobs paid more, they were the first places I sought employment. In Lititz, near Lancaster, I found a job as a laborer for $1.35 per hour, lugging bricks and concrete and digging ditches.

The work was tough, the hours were long, and the humidity was stifling in the ninety-degree heat, but though I felt like quitting on many days, I endured, because I knew the money had to be amassed, if I planned to continue my education.

At the outset of my second year at Piedmont, an outstanding music professor, Mr. Lee Baum, was hired to teach musical instruments, including the cornet and piano. One of the requirements for graduation was to pass an instrumental course of instruction, and he became my cornet instructor.

That craving to learn to play the piano, while at Mt. Lou San Bible Camp, and those two months of lessons my freshman year, really fired up my desire to play the piano more, even though I was engrossed in cornet lessons. With pianos located in most of Piedmont's educational buildings, and the main auditorium of the Salem Baptist Church, where the college classes were held, I had easy access to play them.

Because I improved at the cornet, I had the opportunity to travel to a church in southern North Carolina, where the Piedmont vocal quartet sang, a student preached, and I played a cornet solo.

After the service, we were invited to the pastor's home for fellowship and refreshments. As I opened a bottle of Pepsi, it fizzed over the top of the bottle and over my hand. Instinctively, I thrust the bottle into my mouth to prevent the liquid from splashing on his living room carpet. Embarrassingly, the Pepsi still splattered over it, but worse, the bottle cracked one of my front teeth, which had to be extracted and replaced with a partial plate.

Playing the cornet became more difficult, because I could not maintain a good embouchure that was essential, when I placed the mouthpiece against my lips.

In February, I started taking the second semester of cornet lessons. Partway through one lesson, I abruptly stopped playing, looked at Professor Baum, pointed to the piano near us, and said, "That is my instrument!"

He knew, where my burning desire was, and without any degree of hesitation, responded, "There is the bench." Often I have wondered, what would have transpired in the future of my life had he refused, since the semester had already begun, and I had signed up for cornet instruction. Actually, the administration could have said the same. *It was the Lord's will for a positive response.*

Professor Baum's words-"There is the bench"-ushered in an important new direction in my life. At that moment, I placed that cornet in its case and rarely played it again. Since I needed the brass instrument for college credit for the entire year, he graciously gave me cornet credit!

During that year, I worked about twenty hours a week at a grocery store. In spite of the full load of class work and that job, I managed to practice the piano fourteen hours a week. As I continued to improve, I requested, that I take lessons twice a week and was obliged.

My confidence in the degree program and piano playing certainly was gaining momentum, and I finished that year with good results.

That summer, I again found a school construction job in the Jonestown area. That company employed only men, who joined the union and paid union dues. To show how good the Lord was to me, when I revealed, that I was a college student seeking temporary work, and that I had worked on construction the year before, he agreed to hire me without requiring me to join the union.

On that job, a worker showed me how to push loaded wheelbarrows up ramps, after I accidentally dumped a load of concrete into a sewer pipe, where a bathroom was to be located. I was blessed, not to be fired for that mishap.

One afternoon, the boss had me quickly hide in the toolshed, because a union inspector was looking for anyone, who did not belong to the union. Thanks to the boss, I was not found.

One job that I did was to dig a deep ditch through shale and solid dirt with a pick and shovel, because earth-moving equipment could not be moved into that area. The day that I was to be laid off, another union inspector made his search, and did not spot me in that deep ditch. Again, I escaped having to pay the union dues!

My third year, I continued to take piano instruction from Professor Baum.

A good friend, who had started a gospel mission work in a rented house, knew how I was improving and wanted me to be his pianist and Sunday school teacher. What an opportunity it was for me to teach that class, and gain musical experience for the Lord!

I worked part time in a grocery store. One day I invited a young man, who worked there, to go to the mission. The next Sunday, he came, sat in my class, and heard me teach from the first chapter of John's gospel. He continued to attend, and finally asked Jesus Christ to come into his heart.

At the end of that school year, the mission closed, and the next school year, I worked for another employer. Unfortunately, I did not see that man again. Since I was faithful in my responsibility to tell him about Christ and invited him to come to the mission, a lost one became born again, and I praise the Lord, that we will meet again in the next life.

Another occasion happened at a junkyard, when I needed a part for my automobile. The person who handled the business had the sort of stature, that would give a young man of small frame second thoughts about mentioning the subject of salvation, but I believe the Holy Spirit had different plans.

The Effect of the Gospel Tract

I approached a man who looked very rough.
He was muscled and his frame truly tough.
Telling him about Christ seemed out of the question,
But I trusted God to give me the direction.

He was a worker at a local junkyard
Who looked as though his heart could be hard.
A gospel tract I handed to him,
Sharing how Christ could save him from sin.

I could have ignored him in fear that day,
But with him, I was willing to pray.
There was no proof of a change of heart
As I exhorted him with Christ to start.

Only eternity will forever tell,
If he at the foot of Jesus fell.
But there is one thing I know for sure–
If he trusted Christ, his heart became pure.

The Bible was the center of all of the courses taught at Piedmont. The theology courses I took that year dealt with the life, death, and resurrection of Christ; eternity; separation; prophecy; the consequences of sin; the consequences of not asking Christ to enter one's life; the new birth, which is specifically stated in John 3:3 (KJV) ("Except a man be born again, he cannot see the kingdom of God"); the necessity that baptism be by immersion; the fact that baptism cannot save but is commanded of God once one is saved; consecration; eternal security as stated in 1 John 5:13 (KJV) ("These things have I written unto you that believe on the name of the son of God; that ye may know that ye have eternal life, and that ye may believe on the name of the Son of God"); and the importance of works as stated in Galatians 2:16 (KJV) ("Knowing that a man is not justified by the works of the law, but by the faith of Jesus Christ, even we have believed in Jesus Christ, that we might be justified by the faith of Christ, and not by the works of the law: for by the works of the law shall no flesh be justified"). Those biblical studies prepared me to minister the gospel, and the doors of opportunity continued to widen while I studied for my degree.

On Sunday afternoons, some of us students would hold street meetings in downtown Winston-Salem. Each week, one of us would preach about salvation and that Jesus Christ was born of a virgin, died on the cross of Calvary for our sins, rose again, and ascended into heaven, and when the trump sounds, all who trusted Him will be bodily caught up to Him in heaven.

If those listeners opened their hearts and accepted Him as their Savior, eternity in heaven was secured! How wonderful that one day, I will meet anyone in glory, who trusted Christ on those streets as promised in 1 Thessalonians 5:16-17: "For the Lord himself shall descend from heaven with a shout, with the voice of the archangel, and with the trump of God: and the dead in Christ shall rise first: then we which are alive and remain shall be caught up together with them in the clouds, to meet the Lord in the air: and so shall we ever be with the Lord."

There was a man, who met us on the sidewalk, and begged us for money for food. He saw that we had Bibles, said that he had been faithful reading his Bible, borrowed one of ours momentarily, opened it without thought to a place in the Old Testament, and began to read. As he read, we knew it was a ploy to receive aid for his worldly habit and certainly not lunch. We did not turn down his wish and agreed to go with him to the nearest restaurant, and pay for his meal. Suddenly his hunger must have vanished, for he rapidly departed.

In my preparations, to minister the gospel emphatically and confidently and prepare outlines, how could I ever forget the speech class taught by Dr. Earl Griffith, where we studied how to expound the truths of the Bible by preparing messages, and actually proclaiming them in class?

In one of my messages, I shared that I was raised in Lebanon, Pennsylvania, and received Christ as my personal Savior in the Lebanon High School auditorium. After I finished the message, Dr. Griffith said, "Dennis, I learned years ago, that we raise chickens and rear children." The comment was humorous but true.

The summer of 1957, I found a job in a clothing store in Lebanon. Every Thursday, we would deliver free suits to the veterans' hospital. How thankful I am for those, who fought and are still fighting for our freedom, and for the great facility available for the men and women who have become injured! Every American should have the experience that I had, just to walk those halls and witness the groaning and suffering that I heard and saw. It would cause all to be thankful to our servicemen for our freedom!

Thank you, servicemen and-women, for our freedom!

Evangelist Billy Graham was holding daily meetings at the Madison Square Garden every evening for sixteen weeks. Because New York City is only 150 miles from Lebanon, six of us young people traveled there in my automobile once a week to listen to the four-thousand-voice choir, the magnificent voices of Ethel Waters and George Beverly Shea, and the preaching of the gospel of Christ by Billy Graham.

The final meeting of the crusade, which was held in Yankee Stadium, left the biggest impression on me. One hundred and twenty thousand people filled the stadium, and about twenty-five thousand were turned away.

After the crowd dispersed around ten thirty, we thought it would be intriguing to ride the subway to the Empire State Building to view the city from the observation floor at night.

On the way back to the parking lot, as we were boarding the subway, three of the boys were not quick enough and were left stranded. Ultimately, they caught up to us at the stadium, but a terrible fear occurred in my mind. What if they couldn't find where we were located? Fortunately, that did not happen.

At two in the morning, we started the trip back to Lebanon. An uncontrolled drowsiness developed the farther I drove. I refused to stop and sleep, because I feared our families would have really worried. I kept the window open, and stuck my head outside every few minutes to keep from dozing at the wheel. How foolish I was!

Due to my recommendation, a friend from Lebanon decided to become a student at my school during my fourth year. The winters in Pennsylvania were usually bitter cold, and one of the recreations that he and I enjoyed was ice-skating. We knew that in Winston-Salem there was no chance to ice-skate outdoors, but we took our ice skates anyway. During that winter, the temperature for a number of days was abnormally low. We drove throughout the suburbs and found a pond that was surrounded by weeping willows, causing the sun's rays to be reduced. Ice covered the pond, and we did what probably no other person had done. Unsure of the thickness, we ice-skated and were fortunate not to break through, but it gave us excitement and an amazing story to tell.

The Ice-Skating Feat

A friend and I are probably the only ones
Who ice-skated in the outskirts of Winston Salem.
The city is too far south for ponds to freeze hard,
But one year, that is what happened to one of them.

We were college students whose homes were in the north.
Some thought we were foolish to take ice skates with us,
But with the mountains not too far to the west,
The thought of packing them in the car became a plus.

A small pond in the suburbs
Was shaded by some weeping willow trees.
The weather turned bitter cold that winter
And amazingly allowed the water to freeze.

People from the city could have called us crazy
If they had suspected, what we had planned to do.

Even though we checked the thickness of the ice,
There was a good chance we could have fallen through.

One thing we can say for sure about that feat-
We were fortunate to live to tell about it.
Bravely, we accomplished the dare that cold day,
But we could have been killed lickety-split.

The Appalachian Mountains are about fifty miles west of Winston Salem. Our curiosity got the best of us. Dissatisfied with the probable danger of that city pond, we wondered, if it became cold enough in those southern mountains to freeze ponds, or lakes thick enough to skate. Near Boon, North Carolina, we found a pond, and much to our surprise, we skated.

That school year, Salem Baptist Church and Day School, where Piedmont classes were held, hired me to work part-time as an assistant custodian. The Lord opened that opportunity for me. Why else was I, instead of any other young man from the college, hired, giving me access to the church keys and to all of the pianos? Since the ministry at the mission came to a conclusion and I was hired at the church and Christian day school, I decided to become a member of the church. What a wise decision that was!

While attending the church services from week to week, I continued to see two pianos at the front of the auditorium. The regular pianist played the grand piano, but no one played the upright. I asked Professor Baum, my piano instructor, and also the church organist, who played that upright piano for the services. Without any hesitation, he said, "You will this coming Sunday morning."

All week I spent much time preparing to play the selected gospel songs. Since the regular pianist played the grand piano, I knew that any mistakes would be overshadowed by the organ, grand piano and congregational singing. After I entered the auditorium, Professor Baum informed me that the regular pianist was ill, and that I would play the grand. What a shock that was!

Every Sunday morning at eleven, the great gospel hymn "Grace Greater Than Our Sin," which was the opening theme song, was sung by the congregation and aired live on the radio. As I depressed the sustaining pedal at the base of the piano, my nerves really did work on me. I trembled with panic to the extent that my kneecaps actually shook!

I thank the Lord that I improved in the coming weeks to the extent that I was asked to accompany the Piedmont Bible College vocal quartet on their summer tour, but out of fear that I was not good enough, I declined.

That year was very difficult for me! As a theology major, I was required to take one year of New Testament Greek, and that certainly was no joyride. There was a student in that class who could have taught it, but because he did not have a degree, he had to take the required course with the rest of us for credit.

That man was willing to work with a group of us daily to help us understand what we needed to master, and because of his expertise and my hours of study, I was able to pass the course.

Working at the church was also in my favor. In my pocket I kept a pack of vocabulary cards, and while I pushed a broom from room to room, I would memorize the words and definitions.

Every Greek student had to complete a research paper. One evening, while I was working on the rough draft, the air became very hot and humid. To stay comfortable, I sat at my desk in front of the open window. A weather front created a tremendous gust of wind, and sucked my nearly finished rough draft out the window and into the torrential rain. I knew that all of my hours of work were gone, and would have to be redone else I fail the course.

When the news spread about my plight, there was a great effort from the students to scour the area the next day, hoping to recover any of those papers. Every one of them was found, wet but still readable, and all I had to do was type the rough draft.

Another problem developed. Among that Greek class and the other required courses, three were taught by the same professor. I became so overwhelmed with the workload that I knew something had to give. Since I had a premonition that I would fail philosophy, I opted to fail that course, and devote my time to the others.

I contacted the administration to ask permission to take that course during the summer by correspondence, studying and taking tests by mail. Permission was granted! Had I chosen to accompany the quartet that would not have been possible!

That summer, I was hired by the state of Pennsylvania to count cars in Reading. What a break! The hours for counting cars were from seven until eleven in the morning and from two until six in the evening for the entire summer. Those were the hours most people drove to and from work. During that three-hour period from eleven until two, I was able to study for that failed course and passed with an A.

A transition took place that summer on our land. Mom and Dad decided to tear down our two-story wooden-framed house, and build a brick ranch-style house. Before the change was made, they discussed their plans with my brother and me, since we still lived at home—him all year and me during the summer.

We agreed to live temporarily in the chicken house in the backyard that would be spruced up and livable. To an observer, that move would seem humorous, but we thought the idea unique and fun, and it helped the plans to go forward!

Dad drew up the blueprints, and after he demolished the house, he built the garage, giving my parents somewhere to live there, while the rest of the construction was completed.

Considering my dad did not finish high school and my brother was seventeen years of age, it was astounding, that they did all of the work except for the digging of the basement. I was unable to assist much, because I was working full-time earning money to continue my education.

While I was on summer vacation, no one had taken my place playing the Salem Baptist Church piano enabling me to continue the opportunity. Members of the church and college continued to compliment how I was improving, but the most important member was a student in a music theory class. He was so impressed, that even after he was in that class for three weeks, he advised me to speak to his professor about enrolling, saying I would most likely ace the course. I took his advice and talked to the professor, who could have said it was too late but admitted me. In most classes, that could not have been done.

Immediately, I began to understand the theory and ended the year with an A. Theory in music is learning terminologies, notes, chords, and the structure of melodies and harmonies—soprano, alto, tenor, and bass.

The Lord led me to that music student at the most important moment in my life, because had I not known about that theory class, the next years' events would have turned out differently.

Before that move, I was indecisive as to where I should go, after I graduated from Piedmont. Because my degree was in theology (the study of God and the Bible), I thought I was heading into a pastoral ministry, and was about to apply to Dallas Theological Seminary in Texas to further my studies towards a master's degree.

After talking to class members and even professors, I expressed concern about what decision I should make once I graduated. Someone suggested, that I should apply to Bob Jones University in Greenville, South Carolina, because they had an outstanding music program. With that suggestion in mind, I applied and was accepted as a sacred music major.

I was required to choose a minor in social studies or English, requiring twenty-four semester hours in the area I chose. Both subjects were equally important for preachers, laymen, and teachers of Sunday school and public or private school.

To minor in English was not my wish. Because I did not think that I did well enough in those courses in high school or at Piedmont, I chose social studies. The university had a different opinion. At Piedmont, I had successfully finished two courses in social studies and four in English. Thus, they advised me to choose English, which I wisely did.

In May of 1959, with my mother, father, and brother in attendance, I proudly walked across the stage as a graduate of Piedmont Bible College. For the second time in my life, I slid my tassel from one side of my head to the other, receiving my bachelor of theology degree after five arduous years of study, proving that with God's help and a willingness to put feet to my prayers, all things are possible!

CHAPTER 6

The Next Step

After I graduated from Piedmont, I again did not know what doors the Lord would open for me, though more education seemed inevitable. I really began to think that music was surfacing more day by day, and with my acceptance to Bob Jones University, it even became more of a reality.

I was not overjoyed about having to spend more years in dorm life, and endure more college or university classes and exams, but I knew it had to be done, if I wished to further my music education.

While I looked ahead that summer to more education, I worked in Manheim, Pennsylvania, boxing automobile brakes for shipment. Again, it was the Lord providing my needs before the next step in my life.

In September, with my packed suitcases, I traveled the six hundred miles to Bob Jones University, where the heat and humidity were stifling. The grapes that I had put into the trunk turned into grape juice.

Upon arriving on campus, I realized that it was not at all like Piedmont. City streets existed on Piedmont's property with no privacy from Winston-Salem's population. What I saw as I drove through Bob Jones's entrance were a guardhouse and a fenced-in campus. I was about to find out many more differences, once I stepped into that phase of my life.

In Piedmont, there were four to a dorm room, but I was hopeful there would be only two at Bob Jones. As I entered my room, I disappointedly saw four bunks. Again, I would be rooming with three others with different ideas and habits. I had learned in my five years at Piedmont, that it was crucial to get along and make necessary adjustments.

Because I had a degree, I would be living in graduate hall, where one was not bound by the same restrictions as the undergraduate students. I was permitted to leave campus at any time of the day or night without permission, and was not bound by the eleven o'clock lights-out rule. My roommates and I could study in our room, as long as we wished. It was essential for me to receive seven or eight hours of sleep every night and for the room to be quiet. Their staying up as long as they wished could have created a constant problem, because I was a light sleeper, but we learned to respect one another.

Not far from the dorms was a long building that contained small practice rooms. We sophisticatedly called them the practice shacks. From there, I could hear the cacophony of sounds of different instruments. At first, what disturbed me was detecting the scales and classical music being played with speed and accuracy. A thought struck me: *I will never accomplish such professionalism.* I felt like packing my suitcases and heading back home, because I figured I did not have what it takes, even though, before I was officially accepted as a music-major, I had to play a classical work. I chose Chopin's Polonaise in A b Op. 53.

Instead of burying my head in the sand, I stayed the course, played the Chopin work successfully, and to my surprise, in a month or so, I was beginning to play some of the scales and classics with speed and accuracy, because of the outstanding piano instruction I received at Piedmont Bible College and my determination.

It did not take very long for me to find out, that students were expected to prepare to do the Lord's business. There was no time for foolishness. After six in the evening and until lights-out was study time, and no male was allowed to communicate with any female.

Students who broke rules were given demerits. An accumulation of 150 demerits was cause for immediate dismissal. Infractions included arriving to classes, chapel, and meals late; not wearing a dress shirt and tie at mealtime; complaining about an instructor; using vulgar language; walking on the grass; arriving back to the campus late after vacation; and having a cluttered room.

On one occasion, while I was standing at the dining room table waiting for the prayer, a student said to me, "You forgot to wear a tie." I did not wish for any infractions or reprimands and dashed a distance of about an eighth of a mile from the dining common to my dorm room to solve the dilemma. With sweat dripping from my face, I returned with the tie around my shirt collar, but, frustrated, I was late by a few seconds.

During my three years there, I received eight demerits. I have concluded that that tie episode was the culprit.

For the theology degree at Piedmont, I took music classes, but the main emphasis was biblical studies, which prepared me to do ministerial work. At Bob Jones, the major thrust was about to change to English and music courses. As was true at Piedmont, classes in Bob Jones began with prayer, and the top priority was winning the lost to Christ.

Since I was a sacred music major, I was required to take a class called Preacher and His Problems, which met daily for Bible study, with the stipulation that I had to be temporarily licensed to preach the gospel.

Every Sunday, a group of us would comb the streets of Greenville to present the message of Jesus Christ to streetwalkers. At that time, blue laws were in effect and even though businesses were not open on Sundays, there were individuals, who were willing to hear the good news of salvation.

All of the music classes were taught in the fine arts building, where I learned how to compose music, conduct choirs, teach voice, and play the piano and organ professionally. Much to my surprise, as a post-graduate student, I was permitted to practice on the nine-foot grand pianos in that building. Those are the kinds played by concertmasters.

To become well rounded in my musical education, I was required to study the lives and perform the works of Bach, Beethoven, Brahms, Wagner, and Chopin, just to name a few-and I thoroughly enjoyed it.

The Theory I and II classes that I had taken my last year in Piedmont were a breeze compared to what lay ahead at Bob Jones University. The main thrust in Music Theory III and IV was to learn to write four-part harmony (soprano, alto, tenor, and bass). J. S. Bach was the musical master who was the authority of the rules of writing four-part structure. Two main negatives were not allowed—parallel fifths and parallel octaves. Most likely, a non-musician would not understand what either one is. At the beginning of those courses, I also had no understanding.

When my first assignment was returned, I shockingly saw a D, and on the next three, I continued to receive D s. Realizing that music theory was a *big key* to my staying in the university, I knew I was in trouble, unless I learned quickly how to recognize, where I was making the errors.

After that fourth D, I began to analyze my writings more closely, discovered how to detect those errors, and began receiving A s. What a comeback!

The problem with four negative grades was that they all figured into the semester average. That seemed unfair, but after I understood why I had made the errors, I received a B in both courses!

Playing grew more enjoyable, as I became immersed in a course called Sophomore Piano and in mastering the basics of the organ.

Intermediate Gospel Song and Hymn Playing was a high point of my education. While at Piedmont, I learned through Professor Baum how to embellish gospel songs, but in that class, I zeroed in on improving those two areas. Mr. Ted Smith, who played for the Billy Graham crusades, and the late Anthony Burger, who thrilled audiences in the Bill Gaither concerts were two men who played in an evangelistic style that was taught in that class.

To be well-grounded vocally and be able to direct choirs effectively, I was required to take the choral conducting class, where I learned how vocalists should stand when singing and how to sing with proper tone, communicate the messages in a song with clarity, and execute numerous moves of my hands and arms when directing choirs.

In speech class, I had to memorize and perfectly verbalize three types of readings in front of the class: a monologue, a duologue, and a play. In the monologue, I became one character. An example of a monolog is the famous speech in Hamlet that begins, "To be, or not to be, that is the question." In the duologue, I became two characters, and in the play, five characters.

In the duologue and play, I had to use the dramatic V. Whenever each character spoke, I had to aim my head in the same direction of the speaking character, and use a different voice for each character.

Example:

Mother Father <u>Child</u> Doctor Teacher

I stood <u>here</u> in the middle of the five
imaginative characters and before the class.

The professor proclaimed, that if one memorized by the whole method (repeating over and over from the beginning of the play to the end), in time, one would not forget the lines. My play had five pages.

When I got partly into the play, my mind went blank. Embarrassed, I stood in front of the class. Instead of coming to my rescue, the professor said, "I can wait here as long as you stand there." Much to my chagrin, I sat down in defeat.

Fortunately, she gave me another chance on a later day. With much more practice, I was able to act out the entire play perfectly, and ended that course satisfactorily.

Years later, I was invited to hear a man, who was a professional organ player, who played an astonishing amount of popular music. When I asked him how many songs he knew by memory, he replied, "Over a thousand."

I asked him what method he used to master them. He said, "Block memory."

Since I had never heard of block memory, I asked him to explain the method.

"In music, poems, verses of Scripture," he said, "one should take the first measure or phrase and go over it until it is mastered. Then go to measure two until it is mastered. Next, do not go to measure three. Put the two measures together and then go to measure three. Continue the process until the entire piece is learned."

From that day forward, I learned masses of music and began to play in public very difficult classical numbers!

Year one was a difficult challenge with low scores at the beginning of some of my courses, but I did not let discouragement rule! In life, I learned that quitters are losers.

During the summer of 1960, I was not overjoyed about working on construction in the summer heat again, especially in the Lebanon County area, where it seemed hot enough to fry eggs on the sidewalks. I knew that in spite of the negatives, construction jobs paid more, and I was willing to use my muscles in spite of having sat in classrooms for nine months.

On the south side of Lebanon, a five-story building was in an early stage of construction, with just the steel beams in place. I was hired immediately, and for two weeks did work on the ground floor.

When I started that job, I had no idea, what lay ahead. After two weeks of doing the tedious work on the ground, the foreman told me, that my new boss would be Marty. I was in disbelief, because I knew he worked on the beams, and wondered what I would do, if I were ordered to work on those six-to eight-inch-wide beams as high as eighty feet.

Just before lunch, the news I feared became reality, when I was ordered to go to the third floor at the edge of the building to pour concrete into the column forms. To arrive there, I would have to walk about fifty feet on those beams with a shovel in one hand and a steel rod in the other. On both sides, there would be air from me to the dirt floor below. With one slip off the beam, I could have been instantly ushered into eternity.

Until that day, I had fear of heights. I had to make an immediate decision—be brave or quit with a prayer, that I could find a summer job elsewhere. I chose to take the risk rather than flee.

After nervously using the steps that had been previously welded to the steel structure for access to the third floor, I gingerly stepped on the beam that extended from the vast area that still had no concrete and started to inch my way to the building's edge. Within a few feet, I froze as I glanced at least twenty-six feet below and saw a number of concrete block workers. To make matters worse, there were two ninety-degree turns with no perpendicular posts, where I had to make two midair turns, and trembling with hunger, since it was lunchtime.

When I saw those men, I could have screamed for help, but instead I slowly bent into a hunched position and waddled. I prayed, "Lord, if it is Thy will, help me to return safely."

The columns were steel posts that supported the upper floors. A crane operator hoisted concrete to me in a huge steel bucket connected by a cable. A lever was connected to a bucket that held a half-yard of concrete. Once I pulled the lever, the concrete flowed out of the base of the bucket through a rubber tube, guided by me into the wooden frame. I had the shovel and steel rod to help spread and pound the concrete around the columns to prevent air pockets.

Once the frame was filled, I inched my way back to safety. During my return, I did not stand upright again at any point, knowing that it was only answered prayer that guided me back.

My father worked at the Bethlehem Steel Corporation in Lebanon. Since our hours of work were the same, I dropped him off in the morning, and took him home in the evening.

While we were heading home that evening, I told him about my horrifying experience, swearing to refuse to walk those beams again. He agreed that no amount of money was worth jeopardizing my life, and that I should quit.

Bob, a friend who had attended Piedmont Bible College, was hired on that same job due to my recommendation. The next day, just before I was to tell the boss that I quit, I saw Bob and informed him that that was my last day on the job, and that steel-beam walking was not worth my chancing another moment.

What I expected from him was agreement! Much to my astonishment, he said, "Do not be foolish. Do not quit. Tell the boss that I want to work on the beams with you, and I will give you instructions on how to walk them safely."

Quickly, he started that lesson with a simple question. "What happens," he asked, "when one rides a bicycle, if he goes no faster than one or two miles an hour?"

I replied, "One loses his balance and he crashes."

"The same principle," he said, "applies when walking on a beam. You do not look down. Instead, you must look straight ahead, walk at a good clip, and head to your location. By doing those things, you will not fall!"

That morning, the boss assigned him to walk those beams with me.

For the remainder of the summer, I worked on the beams, lost *most* of my fear, and was complimented by a carpenter, who saw me from day to day and said, "Deacon, you are really becoming an expert up there."

It was a testimony to be called deacon or preacher, because during lunchtime, I was able to tell those construction men about the love of Christ, and their need to accept Him as their very own.

That carpenter owned a farm. When he continued to observe, that I was a faithful worker, he asked me, if I wished to work on his farm over the weekend to bring in peas. I accepted his invitation and earned more cash.

Working with Marty on the beams was an experience in itself. To him, every move was rush, rush, rush! On two occasions, he slipped momentarily, and could have fallen to his death.

On that job, no one wore a hard hat to protect his head from falling objects. Bob's father, who was a construction worker elsewhere, lent me one. One day, after I pulled the lever, the concrete jammed in the rubber tube, gushed over the top, all over the hard hat and my body. I sat in danger, soaked, and was fortunate to make it back safely.

After spending that summer working every day, always one slip away from possible death, I thank the Lord, that my life was spared, but have often wondered, why any foreman with common sense would order an inexperienced laborer to work on beams.

On that same site, a worker did fall to his death in the elevator shaft that was under construction.

Beam Walking

To earn tuition throughout my college years,
I found labor jobs on construction sites.
At one location, where I was hired,
I had to walk steel beams at nervous heights.

There was no protection on those six-inch widths,
Only air between me-and the ground.
I felt like a foolish acrobat,
Knowing with one slip, I would be sidewalk bound.

My job was to fill boxed columns
With concrete unloaded from a crane.
As I did this gut-wrenching work,
I became accustomed to the strain.

Not everyone who worked on that job
Was as lucky to survive as I,
For one man made a fatal mistake
And fell from about eighty feet high.

A building under construction, demonstrating the
kind of beams and heights I had to walk
Photo by Christine Males, wife of Pastor Paul Males Jr.,
pastor of Westlake Baptist Church in Westlake, Ohio

I started my second year at Bob Jones University in a Shakespearean class with the responsibility of reading eight plays. On the very first day, the professor said, "Ladies and gentlemen, I inform you today that this Shakespearean class is not my class. It is yours. I passed this class many years ago. What you do in this class is up to you."

From the outset of that course, I again had a rude encounter. On the very first test, I received a 30 percent. After the second play studied, I received another 30 percent. At that juncture, I knew I was in deep, deep trouble.

I began to realize, I needed to zero in on the lectures more proficiently, and learn the important facts, as she followed the obvious thread of each play.

Because I followed that plan more carefully, my score on test three leaped to 45 percent.

On the fourth test, I received a 60 percent, which to the educators was a low D, but to me it was a 100 percent improvement. Had I ended the course with a D, I would have had to repeat the course with the potential of failing again; take another one in its place, that would have cost more money, time, aggravation, and perhaps not pass that course either; or be forced to drop out of the university.

Thankfully, the scores that I received on the next tests were much higher. What a shock when I made a *95 percent correct* on the final test! With that score, I had a nervous hope for a final grade of C or better.

When it came time to retrieve my report card from my mailbox to learn how I fared in all of the courses that semester, mine was missing, which played havoc on my nerves, especially with the fear of what the Shakespeare final grade would be.

The next day, I could barely turn the mailbox dial. Again, the box was empty. On the third day, the card was finally there. I was about to receive, what I knew would be devastating news. As I opened it, staring me in my face was the Shakespeare final score of C - which was an answer to my prayer!

One of the most beneficial courses I took that year was Advanced Grammar and Composition. At the start of the course, the professor gave a pretest to determine one's knowledge of the rules of grammar. Again, I was jolted with crushing results. My score was 25 percent!

Sitting next to me was a trombonist, who was also a sacred music student. When I told him, that I had such a low score, he indicated that he had a good concept of grammatical structure, and thought it would be in both of our interests to study together.

How miraculous it was that God placed me in that course with an outstanding instructor and that music student with his knowledge of grammar sitting next to me! Perhaps he was the only one, who would have been willing to study with me, or who could have helped me accomplish my goal.

We decided to make that course a game by not making As but by earning perfect scores on every test, and, if mistakes occurred, finding out why.

To accomplish our goal, we decided to study one hour every day and drill diagrammatically the easiest to the most difficult sentences, until we improved our writing skills, and could teach each other *perfectly,* what we had mastered.

I was so determined to improve where I needed help, that I also paid a friend one cent for every mistake I made, if he would explain why I made the error, and have me explain the correct usage to him, until I had it completely understood. One cent in that day was a lot, considering that I only received a few dollars a month from my parents. Part of that money had to be used for dry cleaning and laundry soap. Even to buy a five-cent candy bar was almost impossible.

Intestinal fortitude and determination paid off in that course, because I received an A on the final comprehensive exam.

During that year, I took two very important courses. One was called Instrumentation, in which I created an orchestral work that was played by members of the university orchestra, and another was called Teaching Methods and Materials in Voice. In that methods course, I had to sing before the class, and was given continuous instruction on how to correct vocal problems professionally.

In the summer of 1961, I was hired to work on the same building under construction, where I worked the summer before, but by that time all of the floors were concreted. After one month I was laid off. In disbelief, I again needed to find a job elsewhere. Because it did not matter if Sears, shoe stores, or any company would hire me, I began my search as far as Hershey in my Sunday attire. Just south of Hershey Park, there was a home being built for orphaned boys.

Dressed in those clothes and my Sunday shoes, I applied. The foreman told me he would hire me immediately, if I were not opposed to working in the mud and dirt. I figured I might not have been hired had I headed home to change clothes.

My wage increased from $1.50 per hour to $2.57 per hour. I felt like a wealthy man.

After the second day, I was heading home on Route 322, and inadvertently began passing four cars in a no-passing zone. I glanced in the rearview mirror and saw a state trooper. In panic, I sped to the front rather than attempting to merge in between those cars. For two miles, he followed me, perhaps to see, if I would break more laws, before giving me a ticket that cost me my second day's wage.

Six months later, I received a letter from the state of Pennsylvania, informing me I was on probation. That was the last I heard from the commonwealth of that state!

One month later, I was laid off from that Hershey job and was hired again at that Lebanon site for the wage of $1.50 per hour.

As I began my last year at Bob Jones, I could see the light at the end of the tunnel! All I had left to take in the English program was English Romantic Poets. Musically, I took courses called Hymn Playing, Classical Piano, Advanced Organ, Music in Worship, and Preacher and His Problems. Since I was heading into Christian service, that fall I was required to take Sunday School Administration and completed that course with an A.

In January of 1962, I had finished most of the requirements toward the bachelor-of arts degree and took courses towards a master's degree in pastoral studies. In addition, I was able to practice the piano and organ a total of thirty hours a week.

I was fortunate that last semester to become an usher at vesper services on Sundays and Shakespearean plays and operas. To most, that might not be considered a big deal. For me, it was what I needed to allay my fears of being before three thousand students and guests, who filled the auditorium. I was assigned to stand at the front of the auditorium. As the facility filled on my first day, I became very nervous, and felt as though everyone were staring at me. After a few weeks, my nerves calmed. Until that job, I even trembled in front of smaller groups. That experience was what I needed for what was to come.

One of the requirements facing me was my piano recital. As was true with all performances, memory was a must. I had to perfect three major classical compositions from three areas of history. To make errors meant failure and no degree.

Two pianists performed on recital day. Surprisingly, I was chosen to play first instead of the young lady. As I played the compositions, my nerves became controlled, and I passed the test! The young lady failed, because she could not even finish the first movement of her first piece.

In conjunction with the recital, I had to compose an original composition that had to be played before the three thousand students, professors, and visitors in the Sunday vespers.

Originally, I was slated to be the fourth from the last performer. Just before the vesper service began, I happily learned that I would be first. Again, that was a blessing, because waiting could have caused me to have a nervous breakdown.

While I waited, one of the faculty members was mentally preparing to do a memorized reading. What shocked me was that though he was experienced, like a convict trapped in a prison cell, he shuffled back and forth!

He said, "No matter how many times I perform, my nerves get the best of me."

That statement and his shuffling were not what I needed to hear just before I was to play!

Even worse was that, when I walked on stage, the auditorium lights were shut off and I played under a spotlight. Thankfully, the Lord gave me total calmness!

Even though I had taken many courses related to music, a question continued to linger in my mind. I asked my organ professor, "Do you think, I could ever teach organ?" The two words that he abruptly uttered left an impression that I have not forgotten. He said, "Why not?" On many occasions, I have repeated that response to encourage people with whom I have had contact.

That question began to be answered, when I was required to teach piano to a student from the Bob Jones Academy. The result of that experience was the tonic I needed!

What a privilege it was to be a student in a university that had a super faculty, an outstanding art gallery, an on-campus hospital facility, academic courses, fine arts productions, and well-known visiting artists.

One of those artists was ninety-year-old Charles Weigle, who, with a scratchy voice, sang his masterpiece, "No One Ever Cared for Me Like Jesus." As he sang that song that has been sung in churches and on religious broadcasts since 1932, I doubt there was a dry eye in the student body.

Another artist who stirred even more my desire to master the piano keys was pianist Gina Bachouer, who played Chopin's "Etude Number Eleven." After she finished to a standing ovation, I made a promise, that

I would perform that magnificent work in a concert one day. Many years later, I fulfilled that dream in a piano recital!

To add to my vocal experience, I sang in the university choir, which produced the magnificent "Elijah Oratorio" and Handel's "Messiah," which helped me learn to direct choirs professionally.

In "Elijah," I was a Baal worshipper, who defied God. The director impressed upon the Baal worshippers, that we had to lose our identity by thrusting our hands skyward to Baal with powerful movements. Otherwise, we would have looked totally foolish.

When Elijah prayed to God to send fire from heaven, fire somehow was literally dropped from a point above the stage.

In the "Messiah" concert, we concluded with the "Hallelujah Chorus." I was not in heaven, but it had to be close! Every believer needs that experience.

Five days a week, there was a morning chapel service, which included the singing of gospel songs, vocal and instrumental specials, and inspiring messages by Dr. Bob Jones Jr., Dr. Bob Jones Sr., and other guest speakers including Dr. John R. Rice.

From day to day, I had a craving to have an opportunity to play for the hymn singing in the chapel services, but it never occurred. With hindsight, I am glad, that I was not asked, knowing what crowds did to my nerves.

In January of 1962, a young man from Korea, a transfer student from Columbia University in New York, who studied cinema, became my last new roommate. He had an MG convertible with a top that would not close. While he drove through a rainstorm, the dirty clothes that he had in the backseat became soaked. When he walked in the room, his arms were full of clothes that he promptly dumped on the floor. He kept them there, because in the next day or two he was intending to move into an apartment off campus. A few days passed, and those clothes began to mildew and stink. I really became irritated and wanted to know if any action were happening regarding his living off campus.

After two weeks, the university refused to allow him as a single student and a newcomer to live off campus. With that news, he finally washed those clothes.

He had another problem. Every night at bedtime, he would take off his reeking socks and stuff them into his shoes. In a few days, I decided to surreptitiously watch how long that would continue. Instead of reporting him to the administration, I diplomatically approached him face-to-face about the problem.

I really expected a confrontation, but much to my surprise, he apologized and promised that it would not happen again. The outcome of the ordeals was, that he became a great friend! Imagine what the result would have been, if I had reported him. Being from Korea, he was fortunate to be alive. He and his parents were attempting to escape from the Communists by crawling under a train that began to move, before they reached the other side. Tragically, his parents lost their lives, but he escaped to freedom.

One day, I walked into our dorm room, and there was Steve lying on his bunk with a sword through his stomach. I was stunned and shaking uncontrollably, as I slowly approached him. I moved the bloodstained sword a fraction of an inch, and immediately wondered, why he had committed such a horrible act.

My heart throbbing and my mind racing with thoughts of his harrowing experience in Korea, I rushed to the door ready to scream! At that moment, he stunningly blurted a loud laugh.

As a cinema student, he had borrowed a fake sword that in the center was shaped like a C-clamp, and screwed it tightly to his body. Upon that device, he had spread imitation blood. When I felt that liquid, I knew it was suicide! What a relief, that it was a practical joke, but he pulled it off not knowing, if I had heart problems!

Nearing graduation that spring, I had to decide, whether to come back the next year and continue working toward the master's degree in pastoral studies, or go into full-time work. That decision could have become more complicated, when a pastor from a church in West Virginia came to the campus and interviewed me, with the possibility of my becoming his choir director. He made this amazing statement that he did not allow for mistakes. With that, I knew it was not wise to be a candidate in that church. He most likely did not read 1 John 1:8-10 (KJV), which says, "If we say that we have no sin, we deceive ourselves, and the truth is not in us.... If we say that we have not sinned, we make him a liar, and his word is not in us."

Even though there was uncertainty about next year, I paid a $10 registration fee.

In spite of the many trials throughout my elementary and high school years, my five years at Piedmont Bible College, and the three years at Bob Jones University, it was miraculous, that I was about to receive my second degree. In fifth grade, I completed the year with three courses, failed and the potential of repeating that grade. What a contrast to my last semester at Bob Jones University, where I earned all A s and B s and, amazingly, out of five hundred who graduated that spring, I ranked eighty-seventh, which placed me in the upper 20 percent! I give the Lord Jesus Christ the praise!

That May, I triumphantly received my bachelor's degree in sacred music and English. My father stood next to me after the ceremony and said, "Son, you have accomplished something that not many have accomplished!"

Throughout the years of my college and university life, I looked forward to vacations. As I reflect back to some of those trips, I realize, that I did some inadvisable things. On one episode, I decided to find out how fast my Plymouth would go. I depressed the throttle, until the speed reached eighty-five miles per hour. Abruptly, my right front tire slid into a rut gouged perhaps by rain or traffic. The car began to swerve from side to side, until I lost complete control. Fortunately, there were no oncoming vehicles, and I managed to regain control of my car.

The Piedmont Bible College year ended around the end of May. After I exceeded three hundred miles on another journey, I wished to see, if my automobile would make it to where Route 15 and 29 intersect west of Washington, DC. I knew, there was a service station at that location, but I forgot it was Memorial Day, and the station was closed! With the gas indicator on empty, I knew, I was in trouble for not taking care of business sooner. A few miles ahead, a station was not observing the holiday, and I had that empty tank filled. What a relief!

While I was driving through the forest in no man's land on Route 15 south of Frederick, Maryland, there was a hitchhiker heading north. Because I thought it would be nice to communicate with someone, after being imprisoned in that car for hours, I stopped to ask him, where he was heading. He said he was going to northern Pennsylvania. I agreed to take him as far as the Pennsylvania Turnpike. After a few moments of speaking, he fell asleep, and slept all the way to the turnpike. Later, the thought struck me, that he could have been an escaped prisoner, rapist, or murderer!

The Day I Picked Up a Hitchhiker

While I was driving through Maryland one time,
I approached a man who was walking.
Since he was heading in my direction,
I decided, I wanted company to do some talking.

At the time, I was a college student,
Heading to my home on vacation.
To allow a stranger in my car that day
Could have been complete devastation.

When I hear of all the kidnappings
That have occurred through my lifetime,
I realize, how lucky I was
That I was not a victim of crime.

During that four-hundred-mile journey,
There was no way I could scream for help.
On that stretch of road, where I met that man,
It would have been useless for me to yelp.

My desire on those trips was to make it home as quickly as possible. One Christmas, as I drove from Harrisburg to Lebanon, there were stretches with low-lying fog. In spite of the danger, I drove through those areas without slowing down. The consequences could have been tragic!

A college friend and I traveled the six hundred miles from Bob Jones University after five in the afternoon for Christmas vacation, rather than wait until the morning. He was not insured to drive, so I had to do all of the driving. At about three in the morning, drowsiness developed. The further I drove, the worse it became. Before we arrived in Lebanon, to slow down or stop, he had to push my foot on the brakes. I do not know, which would have been worse-my not stopping to sleep a few hours, or having him drive and have a mishap with his lack of insurance.

CHAPTER 7

After University Graduation

Just after I graduated from Bob Jones University, I was hired, as a laborer for a private contractor, who was constructing homes in the Lebanon area. There, I lugged and nailed asphalt shingles to the roofs, and was a gofer, one who *goes for* whatever is needed, but that employment was about to change.

One Sunday, Mom and Dad invited our pastor and his wife for dinner. While we were in conversation, I informed the pastor, that I had registered to return to Bob Jones University to continue working on a master's degree, but I was completely negative about more preparation, since that would have been my ninth year of professional training. Enough was enough!

Surprisingly, he knew a pastor in northeast Ohio, who was in need of a choir and visitation director. Immediately, he called him, and I was invited to interview for the position at that Baptist church the next Sunday.

The next day, I jubilantly shared the news with the foreman, who wished me success and allowed me time off to go.

On to an unknown church, pastor, congregation, and city, I headed to find out what might be the Lord's will. After a day of sharing my personal testimony, love for Christ, and qualifications and directing the choir and congregational singing, the church decided immediately, that I should start that ministry on Sunday, August 5, and gave me amazing news, that a family, who lived about twenty miles from the church, would kindly open their home for me to have room and board free for three months. I would then have to relocate. How could I thank them enough for that generosity?

When I returned to the construction job, I gave the foreman my two-weeks' notice. Suddenly, I was cognizant, that new challenges were just ahead. I lost that registration money to Bob Jones University, since it was nonrefundable, but there was no disappointment, for I was ready for the new challenge.

On the fifth of August, I began that new experience at that fundamentalist Bible-preaching church. What an opportunity it was from the very start! The pastor was about to leave for a month and gave me a crash course on the responsibilities of pastoral work, which included preaching at Sunday morning, evening, and Wednesday services and on the radio for four Sundays.

At the end of the three months of living with that kind family, I received news that an elderly man whose wife was a member of the church had passed away. Since the pastor was still out of town, I prepared to preach at his funeral. Just before the day of the funeral, the pastor returned and relieved me of that new experience, but he thought it would be appropriate for me to pray at the gravesite.

Once the funeral was over, that family had a real concern about the deceased person's wife living alone, and thought it would be a great idea for someone to live in her home.

Talk about God's timing! The three months of living in the Painesville area was nearing an end, and I needed quickly to find another place to live. The woman and her family allowed me to move there on October 26. This arrangement also included free room and board, and the home was approximately one mile from the church.

By my moving that close to the church, I was able to conduct, what was expected of me with much more efficiency: spending less time and money on transportation, developing the youth and adult choirs to sing His praises professionally, and educating the believers on how to reach the neighborhood for Christ through witnessing and visitation.

One of my responsibilities was to oversee the visitation program, which also involved contacting visitors. A card was given to them that asked for their name, address, telephone number, religious affiliation, and other pertinent information for follow-up calls.

The winter of 1962-1963 was one of the most brutal winters on record in northern Ohio. On December 7, I was driving on Euclid

Avenue when the rain turned to snow. For four consecutive days and nights, the area was pelted with nearly four feet of the white stuff.

After that storm was over, the temperature dropped to zero degrees and below from the second week of December through much of March. Perhaps the harshest day was January 23, when the temperature dropped to nineteen degrees below zero.

The Brutal Low Temperatures of the Winter Of 1962-63

12/11/62	-1°
12/12/62	-3°
1/22/63	-17°
1/23/63	-19°
2/21/63	-8°
2/25/63	-15°
2/26/63	-10°

Daily I knocked on doors with the blistering winds thrashing my face, ready to tell individuals about salvation and the need to receive Christ as their Savior, and to invite them to fellowship in a church, that proclaimed the good news of the gospel.

As a believer, I learned quickly, that one cannot know, what to expect, when the truth of God's Word is presented. The natural man does not wish to hear, that he is lost in sin, needs Jesus Christ as his personal Savior, and faces the consequence of an eternal hell, if he does not receive Him. John 3:16-18 (KJV) says, "For God so loved the world, that he gave his only begotten Son, that whosoever believeth in him, should not perish, but have everlasting life. For God sent not his Son into the world to condemn the world; but that the world through him might be saved. He that believeth on him is not condemned: but he that believeth not is condemned already, because he hath not believed in the name of the only begotten Son of God."

Romans 10:9-13 (KJV) says, "That if thou shalt confess with thy mouth the Lord Jesus, and shalt believe in thine heart that God hath raised him from the dead, thou shalt be saved. For with the heart man believeth unto righteousness; and with the mouth confession is made unto salvation. For the scripture saith, Whosoever believeth on him shall not be ashamed. For there is no difference between the Jew and the Greek: for the same Lord over all is rich unto all that call upon him. For whosoever shall call upon the name of the Lord shall be saved."

A number of visits that I made were absolutely unique. At one home, I was cordially invited in to share the news of salvation. Amazingly, piles of empty cigarette packages and butts were scattered over the entire living and dining room. I was surprised, that they were not discarded in the trashcan.

On one of the visitor's cards, a family indicated, that they were Baptist. I had a premonition, that a visit there would be cordial. The greeting I received blew my mind! After I indicated the purpose of my visit, I was verbally abused by a shouting and cursing man, and feared I would be thrown off of his property.

An insurance agent, who was a member of the church, invited me to visit a family with him. He said that when I entered the home, I would be shocked. As I walked into the kitchen, the stench of spoiled food assaulted my nostrils. Under the kitchen table was a pile of dirt and rubbish that had to have accumulated for months. On the table were dishes with moldy food. Running around the house were four filthy-faced young children.

I expected to see a handicapped parent, who was unable to care effectively for those children. Down the steps from the upstairs, a mother appeared, who had to be in her twenties with no disabilities. How that woman got by with that filth and four young children baffled me!

Along with being in charge of the visitation ministry, I developed a youth choir and directed the existing adult choir.

The first major work the adult choir sang was John W. Peterson's cantata, "No Greater Love." What a blessing to direct the choir, before a full church in that dynamic and heart-stirring music depicting the love of Christ!

That work has to be one of the greatest gospel renditions ever composed.

For Easter, the choir sang another dynamic cantata by Mr. Peterson called "Hallelujah! What a Savior."

In the spring, I became aware of a rumor that was permeating the church, that the pastor was seen smoking cigarettes. Naturally, members would come to me, hoping I would give them the scoop as to his involvement. I would tell them, I knew nothing and would rather not become involved. I knew it was wise to ignore the rumor, and go about the business of reaching the lost for Christ, and improving the music and visitation programs.

In that church, smoking was not acceptable for members, Sunday school teachers, music directors, choir members, deacons, and especially the pastor. With that pastor, I worked every day, and had no reason to believe that he was guilty.

To me, it was not my business anyway, whether he did smoke. That was between him and the Lord, but one day, he approached me, and charged that I might be stoking the problem.

Because the rumor continued to gain momentum, he ordered me into his office and blatantly asked, if I believed he were guilty. I said that I honestly had no idea.

Abruptly he thrust his hands under my nostrils and asked if I detected nicotine. Stunned, I saw yellow stains and smelled the odor of nicotine.

Since I was not about to lie, I told him, that what I detected was the appearance and especially the scent of nicotine. I could have said no to stay on his good side and save my job, but when I did not say, what he wished, another key to my life rapidly developed.

Some time later, he ordered me to go to the basement of the church. There on a table was an enormous pile of what appeared to be cigarette butts. He indicated, that he had asthma, and to control it, he had to smoke those asthmatic cigarettes. That sight on the table really amazed me! This was also the first time I ever heard of such a thing as asthmatic cigarettes.

These questions entered my mind after that episode. Why did he secretly and for a lengthy period of time save those cigarette butts? Why did he continue to deny any involvement? Why not just tell the truth- that he had a problem and needed prayer, or that those were asthmatic cigarettes? I knew the congregation very well by that time, and believed that the people would have helped him through the struggle.

Because I was honest, he really began to blame me for the spreading rumor. Just before the month of May, I surprisingly was given an ultimatum to stay for two weeks and be paid, or be paid outright for two weeks and resign immediately. What a surprise-both that I was let go, and that it was abrupt!

To continue in that ministry any longer, I knew would have been a tense situation. I opted to take the two weeks' pay and resign, and began to wonder, why that ministry for me had ended so quickly, especially it was the pastor and not I who was allegedly guilty.

For one more year, he was continuously challenged by the church about his guilt and was forced to resign. Those members, even though most knew, I had not created his dilemma, believed the Lord set the whole episode in motion, because it was time for him to be relieved of his leadership. Naturally, I was sad, that I became the goat, but that fork in my road of life was for my good.

I was elated, when a member of that church organized a going-away party! His home was flooded with many well-wishers from the church.

The morning of May 5, 1963, was my last day of exactly nine months of a unique and God-led experience. Since the pastor was in his seventies, many had thought, I would become their pastor in the near future. A number of things indicated that. As I said, I preached on the radio and for church services. The visitation ministry grew, which had a direct impact on the growth of the church. Finally, the choir sang outstanding choral arrangements.

The grandmother's granddaughter, mother, and dad, who lived on the west side of Cleveland, visited every Tuesday. After a number of months, I asked her granddaughter for a date. Our friendship grew, as those dates continued throughout the spring.

After one of the dates, I told her I would cease our relationship. Five minutes later, I changed my mind, and said that I would see her the next weekend. She could have refused any further association with me, but thankfully the dates continued.

Because I continued dating a wonderful young lady, who had accepted Christ, when she was in high school, I had a serious decision to make—to stay in Ohio or to return to Pennsylvania. Due to our relationship, my decision was to wait and not make any hasty moves.

Since the morning of May fifth 5 was my last association with that church, I decided to visit the Madison Avenue Baptist Church in Cleveland with Joy and her family that evening.

There are certain dates that are cemented in my mind. Of course, May 20, 1963, was one of the most important ones, for on that day, I took the next step by becoming engaged. Without hesitation she said yes! As soon as that mutual step was determined, my choice to stay in Ohio became confirmed.

With that decision, I knew, it was important to become one, not only in marriage, being born again, but also in church affiliation. It was imperative, that I join a church that proclaimed the gospel of Christ. I made that move, and joined the Madison Avenue Baptist Church. Little did I realize, how involved I would become with that Cleveland church!

A friend of mine, who also graduated from Piedmont Bible College, was holding an evangelistic meeting in a Baptist church in Euclid, Ohio. Joy and I attended that meeting, and afterward, I informed him about what had happened at my former ministry and my present uncertainty. He indicated that his father was the pastor of the Graham Road Baptist Church in Cuyahoga Falls, Ohio, and was seeking a music man for his daily vacation Bible school.

That church hired me to be the music director for those two weeks, which proved to be a total blessing, as I taught those children songs of faith, that were publicly sung at the concluding program.

Every day the pastor invited me to his home for lunch. That was very important, because he handed me two original poems that were put to music by a friend of his. He was not happy with the musical scores, and wondered if I could write better renditions.

At his piano was the beginning of my independent writing of gospel music. Before that day, all of the music I had written had been done under the tutelage of professors, as I worked on my bachelor-of-arts degree in English and music. Those two numbers were written and completed in less than two weeks and to his satisfaction.

It was gratifying to know, that I could develop original ideas without the leadership of experienced writers! That self-confidence grew as I wrote gospel songs and choruses based upon God's infallible Word. The first chorus was "But These Are Written" (John 20:31 KJV), which has been sung in churches for over forty years.

But These Are Written

"But These Are Written"

97

His son not only did evangelistic preaching in other churches, but was also a pastor of a rapidly growing Michigan church, that was searching for a full-time music director. Since Joy and I were preparing for marriage, and thought the Lord was leading us into another gospel-preaching church, we accepted an invitation to interview there.

Even though it seemed as though that congregation would call us, we received a rejection letter. We were very disappointed, but knew the Lord would open the door for us someplace else.

From a human reasoning, I really became concerned about future employment, when a Cleveland area Baptist church did not hire me.

Since I had music and English degrees, I applied for a position in the Mentor and Painesville School Districts with no response from them.

With our wedding facing us within months, I had to depend upon the Lord for a door to open. Knowing that the pastor of the church where I worked, when I had come to Ohio, had believed I was responsible for his problems, I suspected, that he would give employers nothing but negatives about me.

My future father-in-law was a security officer at the Cadillac Tank Plant, located in the building that later became the International Exposition Center in Brook Park, Ohio, next to Cleveland Hopkins Airport, where army tanks were assembled.

At that juncture, two positive events occurred. First, during the summer, I was allowed to continue to live in Joy's grandmother's home without having to pay room and board. Second, Joy's father had a connection for me to be hired at the tank plant once Joy and I were married.

CHAPTER 8

Our Wedding

On September 21 at seven o'clock in the evening, Joy and I tied the knot in the Madison Avenue Baptist Church. What an awe-inspiring, candlelit evening that was, as I saw my beautiful bride walk the aisle, where the wedding party and I stood. There, Pastor Camp joined us the way God intended. Second Corinthians 6:14 (KJV) says, "Be ye not unequally yoked together with unbelievers; for what fellowship hath righteousness with unrighteousness and what communion hath light with darkness?"

After the ceremony, a reception was held in the church. Once the meal and the wedding cake had been eaten, Joy cast the gorgeous bouquet across the back of her shoulders into the grabbing hands of the waiting singles.

A Miracle Encounter

In October of 1962,
At a cemetery near Cleveland, to the west,
I had the honor to offer prayer,
Even though, I did not know the deceased.

The preacher presiding at the site
Was the pastor of a church in Willowick.
Since I was his assistant at the time,
To do this, made me very ecstatic.

What was very important on that occasion
Was the presence of a lovely person!
Her grandfather was the one buried that day,

99

But she would see me again for another reason.

Because of her grandfather's untimely death,
Her relatives made an important case-
That her grandmother should not live alone
And I should move into her place.

After I moved into that grandmother's home,
I began dating her granddaughter.
When we realized, we were meant for each other,
An engagement ring I quickly bought her.

I believe that God had His hand in this,
For the young lady impacted my life.
As the days turned into many months,
Our love grew, and she became my dear wife.

Our united blessed day

After the wedding, we moved into an apartment on the north side of Lakewood, Ohio.

Knowing that I had very little cash and was guaranteed employment at the tank plant, Joy and I took a honeymoon in my old 1941 Plymouth to the gorgeous Schroon Lake and fall-colored Adirondack Mountains in New York.

That trip was met with a problem. The motel where we stayed in Rochester the first night was fine, but after we enjoyed the beauty around Schroon Lake area the next day, we headed south toward Pennsylvania. After the sun set, and it was time for us to find sleeping quarters, there was not one motel seen, as we drove for miles. I really became nervous, since we were in the midst of mountains, forests, and cow pastures on an unfamiliar highway.

Near the midnight hour, we finally spotted a motel sign. Relieved, I turned into a driveway leading to our destination. Of course, we were totally exhausted, and knew we had no choice, but to pay for the night, or sleep in our car along the side of the road, which would not have been a safe situation.

With what we were about to experience, perhaps we should have parked in a secluded area. That motel turned out to be a chicken house converted into a motel. What a crude atmosphere: potbelly stove, aged bed, cramped quarters-certainly not a place for my new bride! Needless to say, it was not humorous, and she never let me live down that ordeal.

The next morning, we traveled to my folks' home in Lebanon, Pennsylvania, where we were greeted by many of my friends with a second wedding reception. Being newlyweds, we appreciated all of those gifts from the Cleveland and Lebanon receptions, since we needed every item that perhaps most newlyweds need.

Once we returned home, we discovered, that the apartment in Lakewood had issues, and after a month, we moved into a brand-new three-story apartment complex in Cleveland.

Since the building was brand-new, we expected no dwelling problems. We soon learned, that we had moved from the frying pan into the fire. Next to our first-floor apartment was the in-house garbage dumpster. Daily, the trash from all of the other floors was disposed of and burned there. Many times, it became stuck, before it reached the first floor, filtering smoke into our home due to the lack of a chimney escape.

To add to that aggravation, the walls and ceiling were not soundproofed. Conversations and noises from neighbors were a nuisance.

Another unbelievable problem was the invasion of spiders that crawled from the air vents.

We signed a one-year lease, but our doctor ordered it to be broken. Thankfully, we were able to move into Joy's folks' home.

As we moved boxes of our belongings into our automobile, spiders by the hundreds crawled out of them.

Thanks to the Lord's provision and my father-in-law's connection, I started the midnight shift at the tank plant as a coolant operator on the first of October. A night person I was not, but I remember nightly walking the hallway to the time clock just before midnight, wondering why I was working in that kind of place with degrees in theology, English, and music.

My responsibility, as a coolant operator, was to lubricate the routers that cut the door and window openings of the army tanks, and to shovel the metal chips, that spread on the floor into a huge container.

After two months, word came to the employees that General Motors had lost its bid to Chrysler Motors Corporation. The change would take place on January 1, 1964. When I entered the complex on November 22, I sadly received my lay-off slip—sad because I was again without a job.

The former Cadillac plant, which became the International Exposition Center, next to the Cleveland Hopkins International Airport

My next move was to stop at the unemployment office to receive unemployment papers, but because I had only worked two months, benefits were not granted. Three months were needed. Working for the church, a private institution, did not allow for that benefit.

When I arrived home, Joy gave me the horrifying news, that President John F. Kennedy had been assassinated in Dallas!

With that bleak news and my unemployment, again I was wondering how we would manage financially, but this time I had the responsibility for two. A man, who was a member of Madison Avenue Baptist Church, recommended that I apply at the Brook Park Ford Motor Plant, where he was a foreman, which I thought would give me an edge.

Following his kind recommendation, I applied and passed the test that was given, but was not hired.

Because my mother-in-law worked at the American Greetings Company, I thought I would have a chance to be hired there, but there was no response, which caused me to wonder, if my areas of education or perhaps the church episode were the reasons.

A representative of High School Born A-gainers (HBA) clubs, who was a member of Madison Avenue Baptist Church, recommended that I apply at their headquarters in New York City. Doing that seemed like a positive opportunity, since I had biblical training. Their objective was for their leaders to go into high schools, have a meeting with each club once a week on school sites for the purpose of winning young people to Christ, and teaching them the Word of God.

I was not hired, and in desperation, I applied to drive regional transit busses in Cleveland, but because I weighed less than 140 pounds, again, I was not hired.

CHAPTER 9

The Call That Started My New Career

Another member of the Madison Avenue Baptist Church, who taught music in an elementary school in the Cleveland Public Schools, called me on December 7 to inform me that she had to leave her position, because she was pregnant and suggested that I visit that school with the potential of taking her place.

That school principal permitted me to spend the day visiting the music classes. The school did not even have a men's bathroom, but that did not dispel the hope, that the position would be mine.

The following day, I had an interview with the head of the elementary music department. During the interview, she handed me a selection of music to sight-read. (Sight-reading is playing a selection for the first time.) I must not have made a good impression, because she refused to hire me. But what she did was recommend that I go to the personnel office and apply to become a substitute teacher. That I did without hesitation and was hired!

On January 6, 1964, I was given a two-day English assignment in the Wilbur Wright Junior High School, and until February 18, I subbed from school to school, wondering, if that would be my future.

The next day, I was given a one-day English assignment in the Lincoln High School. At the end of that day, I was told, that the assignment would continue two more days, because the regular teacher was injured in a boating accident.

Unexpectedly, as I was teaching a class that Friday, the head of the English department entered the classroom without warning and observed me in action. At the end of the day, the school extended the assignment for another week.

The next Friday, the department chairman again observed me. I had a deep-seated belief that good things were transpiring, because that day, the assignment was extended until the end of the school year, which gave me tremendous experience as a beginning English instructor.

The next school year, that teacher returned to work, and I continued as a substitute from school to school.

In the middle of November, I was assigned for one day to the Newton D. Baker Junior High School. A teacher noticed my rapport with the students, and wondered why I was not a classroom teacher. I said that I was not certified in Ohio.

As a result of his recommendation to the principal, the principal contacted the personnel office, and recommend that I be hired full time.

Thanks to them, on November 30, I became a full-time English teacher at the Max Hayes Vocational School, an industrial school that trained high school boys and adults in electronics, carpentry, plumbing, auto mechanics, and foundry.

On that day, the principal told me, that he had looked over my credentials, noticed that I had a degree in English and music, and thought it would be super, if I developed a boys' glee club in the only Cleveland school, that had no music program. Naturally, I accepted the challenge.

The school's courses were designed to prepare half of the young men to go into an industry with hands-on experience in the morning and the other half in the afternoon. While in the school, they would take the standard courses, such as English, mathematics, science, social studies, health, physical education, driver education, and specialized courses.

Along with two English classes during the morning and afternoon, I was also assigned one choral class in the morning and one in the afternoon. To fill each choral class with students, at the beginning of the semesters, I recruited students from the study halls, who were willing to sing. Most, or perhaps all of them, could not read a musical note.

Once the classes were filled, I had to determine their voice range and blend those voices into melodic and harmonic tones. For special programs, such as assemblies, Christmas programs, and commencements, the two classes joined together and sang on three-tier risers, before the entire student body, faculty, and visitors.

Enthusiastically, they would come to school a half hour early to practice every day.

Wishing to look sharp for the performances, they sold candy bars to garner enough money to purchase sixty blue blazers.

In a high school setting, and with boys preparing for industrial careers, if those young men appeared or sounded foolish singing in front of their peers, they would have been laughed at with scorn. That never occurred! What a privilege it was to develop, direct, and hear them in concert.

Every year, an all-city chorus performed in the Severance Music Hall, the home of the Cleveland Orchestra. Outstanding student singers from all of the Cleveland high schools were chosen yearly to sing in a massive concert. An individual would sing a prepared solo before judges, who would rate his vocal skills on a scale of one to five. One of the boys from the glee club was chosen and sang a gospel song called "Peace I Leave with You," earning a number-one rating.

All first-year teachers at Max Hayes had to be initiated. The event took place in a secluded sports complex. I had no idea what was involved in the initiation, but it did not take long to find out once the meal was served. Upon my plate, were placed two slices of bread with cardboard between them. In my glass of water was a live minnow. It could have been worse, because some of the teachers had to sink their heads into a tub of water to retrieve apples. While under the water, one of the veterans swatted the victims' rear ends.

Everyone who teaches in Ohio has to be certified. As long as I successfully completed the required courses in three years, I was allowed to continue to teach seventh through twelfth grade English and music. After three years, I was certified, and because I was successful, I was exempt from taking the course called practice teaching.

As I taught English at Max Hayes, I really appreciated the training I had received while earning my degree in music and English at Piedmont and Bob Jones University. The grounding in that advanced grammar course and the fruits of working with that friend daily were the reasons I was able to help those young men to understand why good writing was important and that understanding the rules of grammar was imperative to improve their reading skills. I also became cognizant, that if they could teach what they learned, they *understood it*!

During one semester, there was a professor from Baldwin Wallace College, who came to our school to teach an in-service course called Inner Action Analysis. That class, which met after school hours, really made me think about how much time during a forty-minute class I lectured, how much participation came from the students verbally, how many silent moments there were, and how much confusion occurred. He emphasized, that if lessons were well prepared, the students would hopefully leave every class understanding the material.

From the outset of my teaching, I believed it was imperative to let the light of Jesus Christ shine in my life. While teaching, my obligation was to teach the required courses of study, but that did not prevent me from sharing my faith with faculty members or students during lunchtime, between classes, or whenever an opportunity presented itself.

On the Fourth of July, 1969, a possible tornado ripped across northern Ohio during a fireworks celebration. Numerous people were injured or killed from flying debris and downed trees.

One of the fruits occurred a few days later, when I received word to go to the hospital to visit one of my former students from Max Hayes, who had been seriously injured in that storm. He wanted me to visit and pray with him. How often does that happen in a public school? Because of that request and visit, I was reminded of how important it is to tell about Christ and be His gospel witness.

While at Max Hayes, I also became active as a member of the Madison Avenue Baptist Church as the high school Sunday school teacher, youth director, and member of the adult choir.

As a Sunday school teacher and youth leader, I was impelled to dig deeper into God's Word and stress to those who might have been unsaved to make the most important decision of their lives—to open their hearts and accept Him as their Savior, feed upon the meat of His Word, and impress upon believers to share their faith.

Adding to those responsibilities, I accepted the position of assistant choir director. For the next five years, the choir sang under the leadership of Mr. Syphers during the Sunday morning services and me in the evening services.

That period of time became very important, because I was young and learned valuable lessons from a man who had gone through hard knocks as an experienced leader! I was like a rookie quarterback learning the system by observing men, who had been there.

Things also changed in my church responsibilities, because I was a trained choir director and became too bogged down with all of my duties. The church wisely relieved me as the Sunday school teacher and youth director.

Since I was able to devote more time to musical preparation, the choir began to sing major works for Christmas and Easter and choral selections every Sunday.

How our lives really changed with the births of our three children, Michael, Jeffery, and Lori. Having two boys initially, Joy and I were thankful. We had a wish for number three to be a girl. Lori's birth came as a complete surprise, because of what happened in the waiting room.

A man who had two boys also wanted a daughter. When the nurse entered the room, she said, "Congratulations, you have a son."

Believing she was talking to me, I began to move toward the delivery room. In a few moments, I was shocked to learn that the baby was born to the other family. Two minutes later, the nurse returned to welcome my daughter to our family.

I was so stunned, that when I called my parents in Pennsylvania to give them the news, I could not speak without choking up for about ten minutes.

Before Lori was born, I bought Joy a bouquet of dainty roses, started one of the stems by placing it into the ground, put a glass jar over it, and kept the ground moist for a year. It rooted and is still living after forty years.

That never-dying rose plant

To My Daughter on Her Twenty-Ninth Birthday

When I learned my wife was pregnant,
I bought her a dainty rose plant.
With a scissors, I cut off a stem,
And planted it in the garden.

By placing that stem in a well-watered plot,
I wished it would not die in that spot.
With a glass jar over the top,
I rejoiced that its leaves did not flop.

I watched with a satisfaction
And a sense of gratification
When after thirty years of growing,
Its life shows no sign of slowing.

The rose reminds us to this day
Of the love given in a special way
Of a fun-inspiring daughter
Who has blessed us with years of laughter.

That bush finally died in the spring of 2013 after forty-four years!

CHAPTER 10

The Unexpected Transfer

Before 1969, the Cleveland Board of Education made a change in policy that would affect me. For years, the school year had been divided into semesters A and B. Students started their first grade education either in September or January, depending upon their birthday. Those who started in September would graduate in June, and those who started in January would graduate in January.

The ripple effect reached me in January 1969, when there was a massive reduction of students-there was no start of a tenth grade class, and the graduating seniors were gone. I was notified that I was to be transferred.

The transfer affected many teachers throughout the entire school system. With anxiety, I called the board and learned that I had more seniority than the other teachers, which gave me a choice of schools. How fortunate I was that Lincoln Junior and Senior High School was where I was transferred, because I knew most of the teachers and office staff.

For the first three years I was a teacher, I had to take three college courses a year to be certified in Ohio. Those courses came with tuition costs, leaving me hundreds of dollars in debt. Lincoln was in an area, where there were enough low-income families, that the government made it possible that as long as I taught there, the entire debt would be paid. Because of that transfer, God supplied that need, when my income was meager.

That cold, sunny January, while I was nervously driving east on Clark Avenue to my new assignment, the air became saturated with the foul odor from the steel mills. Immediately, I wondered whether this odor was going to be a daily occurrence, since the mills were only about a mile east of the school. Fortunately, when the wind blew from the other directions, the school was free of that odor.

In conjunction with the odor, I quickly learned how filthy the air was from those mills. The fresh snow that covered the earth in the morning would be black with soot by late afternoon.

After I entered the building and received my assignment, I headed to my seventh-grade homeroom. The first contact I had with students in a room with paint-peeled pipes hanging from the ceiling was a bloody fight between two students. What a greeting compared to Max Hayes, a high school where fights were rare!

After that bloody fight, I wondered why the Lord had put me into the life that lay ahead. Realistically, I had to learn not to question His way!

My last class of the day was located in a room next to my homeroom, where our voices echoed off the walls, and also had an unsightly ceiling and low hanging pipes.

Classes were labeled with skill levels one through fifteen. Section one was the honors group. That first English class was section fifteen. The greeting I received was horrid with very little, if any, appreciation for education. Many in the lower-level classes seemed to have more emotional problems due in part to academic issues.

I informed the mathematics chairman, who had all of his classes in a much better location, of my dilemma. Since his room was available during the same period, he made it possible for me to be transferred to that room. With his assistance and a non-dungeon-like room, I was able to teach more efficiently. It was astounding that classes after lunch, the students' candy-filled bellies or a bad atmosphere affected their decorum. Even though that teacher had come to my aid, again I was frustrated that I was severed from the high school comfort zone, where I had been the director of that sixty-member boys' choral group, where the higher student maturity level in most of the English classes was obvious, and where I had believed that I probably would be until retirement.

The shock of being transferred to Lincoln began to subside, especially when the Lord put me in communication with the school's skilled band teacher, who inspired me to compose more, and helped me to further my understanding of the intricacies of musical compositions.

About the same time, I learned that the secretary of the Madison Avenue Baptist Church had written poetry. A growing desire welled within me to compose a major original work. To her I expressed my wish. In time, she greeted me with a biblical idea: why not develop a unique missionary cantata?

A cantata is a major work of music based upon the Bible. The theme of the cantata she suggested was "Go Ye! Go Ye! Was Our Savior's Cry!" In a few months, the poetic concepts were conjured up, and the musical scores were begun, with the texts based upon the Old and New Testaments of the King James Bible.

As we collaborated and the rough draft began to develop, I indicated to the band teacher, what we were constructing. He even became involved, spending moments before the start of each school day critiquing and aiding in the perfecting of that work.

Often what I thought was a logical idea was throttled due to what he considered to be a weakness. At times, I even became frustrated with his suggestions or with my ideas, but I studied them and usually made more profound adjustments.

I certainly appreciated his input, and by working as a team, we finished the cantata in about one year. On November 19, 1978, the Madison Avenue Baptist Church Choir sang it before a packed church.

In that old Lincoln High School, I was fortunate to be assigned to teach all day for a number of years in the same room, which was opposite an open courtyard and close enough to the head of the English department chairman's office that he could hear me teach, though I was unaware that he could hear my instruction.

The English department heads had always taught the honors classes. What a surprise that he heard me teach through those opened windows, and had enough confidence in my skills and rapport with the young people that he asked if I wished to teach the honors classes for the next two years! He said that he needed a reprieve.

Because I accepted the challenge, permission was granted by the board of education's English department.

Any of the school's English teachers could have been given the opportunity, but he did not give them consideration. What an honor!

A number of years later, he accepted a transfer to another junior high school as department head. He really urged me to transfer with him. After I pondered over what to do, I decided there was no logical purpose in transferring. For one, it would have affected my status in seniority. Secondly, it would have been a lateral move from one junior high to another, and thirdly, I would have left a familiar establishment for the unknown.

I sought advice from one of my colleagues, who advised me to write down all of the positives and negatives. If there were more positives than negatives, it would most likely be unwise to make the move. I came up with only one positive—having the same department head. I, therefore, stayed put.

In the early 1970s, I studied a book about teaching. One of the chapters explained how one could master the meaning of an enormous number of words quickly by using an acrostic approach. Because of the idea, I decided to spend months developing sets for me to build my own vocabulary with power! Since those words, sentences, and definitions stuck so quickly in my mind, I was convinced that I could use the sets in my classes. In a very short time, I found out that it was also an easy and astonishingly *fun way* for my students to build their vocabulary. Every year, I taught the classes approximately 150 or more difficult but practical words.

I was overwhelmed by how quickly the children became involved. Whenever they found words being taught in their readings from the newspapers (not books, encyclopedias, or dictionaries), they would cut out the sentences, underline the words being taught, and bring them to the classroom, where I displayed the sentences on huge, white, twenty-four-by-thirty-six-inch poster cards. No sentence from the same source could be duplicated. Incentive and excitement to read increased rapidly, as the students brought in literally hundreds of the taught words.

What amazed me was that when I encountered former students years later, they would thank me for the impact that those sets had on their reading and writing!

A young man was working on a utility pole. As I was heading toward the bank, he shouted, "I know you! You are Mr. David Fox." I responded, "I am Mr. Fox, but my first name is not David." "You are not David," he said, "but you are Mr. Fox. You were my English teacher ten years ago. I still remember all of those words, and memorizing them your way was fun!"

After I left the bank, that man was standing with his partner and said, "Please tell my friend about your vocabulary method!"

The Madison Avenue Baptist Church men enjoyed meeting at a Christian campground near the Pennsylvania border once a year. A young man from another local church was invited to go on one of the bus trips. He told me his name was Joe, and that he had been in one of my English classes approximately ten years earlier and also still remembered the sets! During the two-hour trip, he proudly verbalized those sets completely from memory.

Mr. Wilson was one of the principals who was impressed with the success I was having with the classes, and recommended that I quickly bring to a conclusion the development of my book and seek a publisher!

There were college students and even an attorney who visited my classes and could not believe that even kids, who were negative about education, were completely enthused about learning the words.

A ninth grade girl was negative and an academic failure before she entered my class. When she was in tenth grade, she returned to the school to show me her report card. I was shocked to see all A s and B s. She told me that it was my way of teaching diagramming and that vocabulary method that made her life positive.

As I taught grammar during the early years of my career, I concluded that diagramming should help more than just studying rules from a textbook. The development will prove that one's construction of a sentence is grammatically correct. I also had them learn the seven patterns of English:

1. Noun + verb: John ran away.
2. Noun + verb + noun: John hit the ball.
3. Noun + verb + noun+ noun: John gave Jack the ball. John painted the ball red.

4. Noun + linking verb + noun: <u>John</u> <u>is</u> a <u>teacher</u>.
5. Noun + linking verb + adjective: <u>John</u> <u>is</u> <u>handsome</u>.
6. Inverted sentence: There <u>is</u> <u>money</u> available.
7. Question: <u>Where</u> <u>is</u> <u>John</u>?

When I began to see the results of my approach, I continued to expand the process on overhead transparencies. One day, as I taught a seventh grade class, one of the students blurted out this statement: "Mr. Fox, we are doing so well at learning your method that you must put your ideas on paper. What you have developed is a self-teaching plan that we can study at home."

As a result, I set in motion to develop my program to include transferring what I had on transparencies to 8.5-by-11-inch paper for the students to study independently. This produced unbelievable results.

Each student I encouraged to go to the chalkboard and repeat the concepts *in front of their peers* until they knew perfectly what I taught. In other words, it was hands-on experience.

Perhaps one of the most gratifying of my English-teaching experiences occurred one year when over twenty-five of my eager inner-city students were so willing to master grammar that they met me *before school* every morning at eight o'clock to perfect their understanding of the eight parts of speech; simple, compound, complex, and compound-complex sentences; independent and dependent clauses; subjective, objective, and possessive cases; the conjugation of the six tenses, infinitives, gerunds, and participles *with a compassion to teach others what they learned and apply all of these areas to perfect their original writings and read with understanding and without frustration.*

There were four students who perfectly diagrammed sentences that were located on a page near the end of their textbook, which ranged from simple to very difficult, with complete understanding of the grammatical position of all of the words, phrases, and clauses in those sentences. They willingly sacrificed their time *to join and teach* those students who had difficulty, so that they could also master the grammar and even teach those concepts.

In my possession, I still have the completed pages done by a ninth grader, Ivan, who was one of the four students, who became my helpers.

After he graduated from high school, he surprisingly came to me one morning to ask permission to speak to my six classes, and advise them to listen to and master my ideas, because as a result of what he had learned, he received a *$50,000 scholarship* to Case Western Reserve University in Cleveland, Ohio.

In time, I would like to take that principal's advice, and have my grammar and vocabulary books published, so that present and future generations can master those concepts as easily as my students did.

I was fortunate to mentor future English teachers from Cleveland State University and Baldwin Wallace College to fulfill their practice teaching obligation. About twenty years later, at a meeting of Cleveland English teachers, I met Pat, who was one of those mentees. She thanked me for the professional assistance I gave her before she graduated.

Naturally, not all of the students in the school or my classes were scholastically minded! During my first few years in that old four-story building, a number of negative incidents transpired. One day, the fire alarm sounded. It was a common stupidity for culprits to pull the fire alarm as a joke. In a few moments, the persons in charge would assume it was a false alarm and stop the ringing. This time the ringing continued.

A teacher rushed to the third floor, shouting, "The second floor is on fire! Move to the stairwell and out of the building quickly!"

It was no joke. Someone had poured a flammable liquid into a room on the second floor, destroying that room. On my way down the stairs, I saw that the entire second floor was filled with smoke. Had we on the third floor stayed a few moments longer, our lives could have been snuffed out!

Every year, there was at least one major student disruption due to gang confrontations. During one incident, the entire student body exited the building, ready for what appeared to be an all-out brawl.

Some of the worst fights were between females. Two literally pulled a glob of hair out of each other's head.

In any such altercations, I did not attempt to interfere; it was not worth putting myself into harm's way. That was why security guards were usually visible.

One day, a young man who was absent from my class decided to join two of his friends in robbing a nearby home. One of the children who lived in that home, learned about their sinister plan, and instead of informing his parents or the police, stayed home from school and waited for them with a shotgun. When they kicked open the front door, he opened fire and killed my student.

The next day, his class sat stunned, as they glanced at his empty chair. Moments ticked by with dead silence. I, too, was speechless. With concern, I stepped into the hallway to seek advice from another teacher, as to what I should say.

I do not remember what advice she gave me, but when I returned to the room, my students were crying and talking about the horrible catastrophe. What the students needed was for me to allow them a moment alone to relieve the tension!

In the early seventies, the board of education planned the construction of a new high school at West Thirtieth and Meyers that combined West and Lincoln High Schools. The two junior and senior high school buildings continued as junior high schools.

The new school's name became Lincoln West High School, combining the two former names. When construction was complete, every teacher from the old buildings was given an opportunity to transfer there. To do so, one had to compose a letter indicating that desire.

I had a real concern, as to what I should do, because I was more satisfied with my present location. Even with that concern, I did compose a letter three weeks after the deadline, thinking that the problems in the high school would be minimal.

Perhaps because I was late with the letter, I was not transferred, and had I been, I believe the move would have been a mistake.

Before the high school students were transferred, teachers had to float from classroom to classroom, because of the huge population in each school. Once the high school students were moved to the new school, the population at my school was drastically reduced, enabling me to instruct in the same room all day. That gave me complete control of the chalkboards, and all class materials could remain in a file cabinet.

The teachers in the new school had to share rooms.

At the beginning of the 1977 school year, a professor from Baldwin Wallace College in Berea, Ohio, came to a faculty meeting to introduce a program called Teacher Core, a master's degree program for just our school's teachers. The meeting was voluntary.

Because I had studied for eight years at Piedmont Bible College and Bob Jones University, and completed numerous hours of courses for Ohio certification, I decided not to attend.

While I was walking through the school library that day, a teacher asked me, if I were going to attend that meeting. Emphatically, I said, "No way!"

That concerned teacher had a different opinion as to what I should do, took me by my arm, and said, "Yes, you are!"

How thankful I was that she had that concern, and that I changed my thinking and went to the meeting!

When I entered the room, I saw the professor, who had taught an in-service course at Max Hayes Vocational School called Interaction Analysis. He also was the head of the Education Department at Baldwin Wallace College.

Again, the Lord put me in the right place at the right time! I did not have a master's degree, and was about to learn how convenient it was to earn one. Two-thirds of the courses were taught at Lincoln after school and one-third at the college. What was even more amazing was that two-thirds of the courses were free!

I decided it was an intelligent decision to stay, and at the end of the first course, I had earned an A!

It was a grueling year and a half, since I had a family, taught daily, and was the choir director at the Madison Avenue Baptist Church. In fact, while I took a course called Educational Research, I took time off as the choir director.

I still remember the relief that overwhelmed me, after I passed the comprehensive exam and completed all of the requirements for the degree!

On June 9, 1979, in the Baldwin Wallace football stadium, with my wife, three children, mother-in-law, and parents in attendance, I proudly walked across a temporary stage and received my master's degree in education.

The next day, I took it to the Cleveland Board of Education to show that the work was finished and received an immediate wage increase.

Of the thirty teachers who worked toward the degree, I was the only one to receive it that year.

My wife and three children had a reception in my honor at our home. Many of our friends and neighbors came to congratulate me and enjoy the refreshments.

Finney Stadium, where I received my master's degree

CHAPTER 11

The 1980s

Times were not easy, as I continued to teach English in the 1980s. Every three years there was a constant threat of strikes, when contract negotiations were in progress.

At the beginning of the 1980 school year, that threat became a reality, when the teachers went on an eleven-week labor dispute. With three children and a wife, I certainly wondered from where the finances would come, though I knew the Lord would provide my needs as promised in Philippians 4:19 (KJV): "But my God shall supply all your need according to his riches in glory by Christ Jesus."

My family

A company called Man Power hired me to go on short-term assignments, that came about by businesses needing short-term labor.

On a one-day assignment, I received $2.01 per hour to help load a semi-truck with old shelves from the courthouse in Cleveland.

A cabinet-building business hired me for six days. While there, the assistant manager and I had lunch at a nearby fast-food establishment. An occasion like that gave me an opportunity to socialize and share the gospel of Christ.

He said that he was from Chicago, was married, and had one child.

After the lunch break, I saw a number of policemen heading toward the open door. When they saw me, they asked if I knew a person with the same name as the assistant manager. Instead of revealing information, I wisely located the manager.

A few minutes later, I saw that assistant handcuffed and led away by the officers, because he was wanted in Iowa for grand larceny and was on the run.

Perhaps he was not from Chicago and had no child or wife. I could have been in danger on that lunch trip.

Even though the pay was meager during the eleven weeks, I worked on various other jobs, met many people in other fields of labor, was able to let the light of Jesus Christ shine in my life, and the Lord did supply our needs, when times were really difficult.

I had the opportunity to give individual piano instruction. In the English department at Lincoln Junior High, one full-time instructor was also the choir director of the world-renowned Singing Angels in Cleveland, which consists of 150 young people and sings yearly on television, in many cities in Ohio, and worldwide. When I informed her of how outstanding four of my students were, they were tested and chosen to accompany the organization. One played in China, Japan, Mexico, and for United Airlines executives in Boston, before Congress, and most likely for the president of the United States.

The second student could have accompanied them on a tour of the United Kingdom, but did not have the finances for the trip. When she quit at fifteen years of age, she began to teach six students.

The third student took lessons for one hour a week for two years. The family did not own a piano or a keyboard. At the conclusion of the two years, her parents purchased a piano. Three months later, she was chosen to accompany the Singing Angels training group.

The fourth student became an accompanist in his senior year. With that organization, one may not continue with them after high school graduation. Had he joined them a few years earlier, he too could have gone on worldwide tours.

Since I had received Christ as my Savior in 1952, the Lord had changed my outlook on life, and I could not ignore the need to share my hope of eternity with others. There was a young man in high school by the name of Harrison with whom I shared what Jesus Christ did and his need to be born again.

Over thirty years later, he called to rejoice with me that he could not forget the words I had uttered from God's Word, and could not reject Christ any longer, and thanked me for his newfound faith. He said that when I spoke to him about Christ, he had no idea what "born again" meant.

He wrestled with the conviction that he needed Christ, but what a tragedy it would have been, if he had continued to harden his heart, and left this life in a lost condition! Perhaps there are those who read this book, who are in the state that he was. Anyone who had accepted Christ can rejoice with Harrison that there is no greater joy than a life with Jesus Christ and of the knowledge of one's destiny.

That call made me realize how important it is to spread the seed of God's Word. We will not know how many have been influenced or won to Christ, because of a word of testimony or the giving of a gospel tract, until we see Christ. Second Timothy 4:2-5 (KJV) says, "Preach the word; be instant in season, out of season; reprove, rebuke, exhort with all longsuffering and doctrine. …But watch thou in all things, endure afflictions, do the work of an evangelist, make full proof of thy ministry."

I might meet numerous ones in heaven with whom I shared the gospel, who at the time were confused or rebellious, but because of the convicting power of the Holy Spirit, were later saved. What would have been the consequences, if I had kept the joy of my salvation quiet.

I attended our fortieth class reunion with sincere reservation, thinking that there could be drinking and smoking at the fire hall, where the event took place. At first, I was unaware that Harrison was in charge of the event. He most likely was influential in inviting a man and wife who sang songs of faith. I left that evening rejoicing!

While I was teaching regular English classes in the 1983 school year, the head of the English as a Second Language Department became convinced that I would be excellent teaching English to children who entered our school from other countries with little or no knowledge of English. For the next ten years, that is what I did.

About the same time, a social studies teacher gave me about one hundred blank X-ray negatives that I used with an overhead projector, and became a valuable visual aid to teach the alphabet, numbers, finances, grammar, reading, writing, and conjugation and to show artistically with permanent markers scores of practical objects, such as things in the kitchen, dining room, bedroom, and bathroom; parts of a bicycle and an automobile; and tools.

From those and other areas of interest, the students constructed sentences.

What a privilege and enjoyment it was to witness their quickness and eagerness to improve!

One youngster came from Mexico and could not understand any English. His transformation from week to week was incredible. Because of his dedicated studying, he aced every test I administered.

Another student came from Central America in November. In February, his mother paid me a visit to congratulate me for the progress he had made in just four months and wondered what methods I used.

Every English as a second language (ESL) teacher has to become ESL certified. After three years of successfully teaching in that area, I was certified and about the same time was granted permanent certification in all of my subject areas without taking further college courses.

Since the transfer of January 1969, I thought I was secure at Lincoln with seniority. At the beginning of the 1987 school year, I entered the school with the disturbing news from the union representative of our building, that I had been transferred!

"No way," I said. "I have more seniority in this building, certification in four areas, and a master's degree. That has to be an error."

It was a fact, but encouragingly, I had the choice between a middle school and a high school.

The principal allowed me to take the day to go to both schools to give me a chance to determine which school was my choice.

After visiting the middle school, I was convinced the high school would be better.

Quickly, I called the board to reveal my decision, but by that time, it was already decided that I would start the next day in the senior high school.

Perturbed, I fought the transfer through union representation. I remember sitting in the superintendent's conference room, where the union representative and I presented why the transfer was illegal.

The superintendent agreed that the move was illegal, but said I would have to wait until January to go back to Lincoln.

I remember having to use a textbook with no teacher edition. In every class I taught throughout the years, teachers had a teacher edition with suggestions for teaching the units and answers to the exercises and tests. In other words, I was on my own!

In an eleventh grade class, a physically strong young man had no respect. After I ordered him out of the class, he picked me up and threw me to the floor. Luckily, I was not injured, and he was suspended for a period of time. When he returned, he gave me no more grief.

During one of the class sessions, a character from outside the building heaved a heavy concrete chunk through a window and just missed hitting one of my students.

In the cafeteria after school, while the English department had a meeting, a student was chasing another student with a car jack. After the meeting, I saw the one who had been chased sitting in the office with blood covering his face.

After facing negatives like that and having to teach in an unfamiliar program, I was a relieved, when I returned to Lincoln.

At the Madison Avenue Baptist Church, while Pastor Hussey continued to teach and preach God's Word, I continued to direct the choir until the late eighties, when the Lord had different plans.

In 1985, Pastor Hussey unexpectedly resigned after twenty-three years of fundamentalist gospel preaching, teaching, and singing in the choir. I will never forget his resonant bass voice, especially when he sang "O Holy Night," which occurred in one of the cantatas. He communed with members of the church and visitors with dignity, and his messages and spiritual leadership were sorely missed.

After his resignation, the new pastor believed it was my time to step down, which allowed him to appoint the principal of the Christian day school that was housed in the church to be my successor.

My wife and I believed it was necessary to move on to another opportunity, since he believed I was no longer effective. It did not take very long until Joy and I became involved with the Mid-Brook Baptist Church (now called Abram Creek Baptist Church) in Brook Park, Ohio.

After we had been attending for several months, a member said to me, that we needed to hang our hats in a church that preaches the gospel of Christ and obeys His precious Word. I knew after that advice, that it was the correct time for us to join. We then could recommend others to follow our example, come to "His" church, learn the truths in God's Word, and, if not born again, accept Christ as their Savior!

After Lori graduated from high school in 1987, she attended a local university for one year but realized that the courses she needed for a degree in photography were not available there. Another university refused to accept a transfer, because she was not in the upper third of her high school class, but she was accepted into the photography department of Ohio State University and passed the mathematical entrance exam, escaping having to take any mathematics classes.

Throughout her stay at OSU, several unimaginable things happened. On the seventh floor of the dormitory where she lived, a helicopter unexpectedly flew next to her window. Later we were informed that it was traveling to an uprising near the campus.

During one of our weekend visits, our elevator stopped in between two floors, and we had to leap a number of feet to safety.

While we were taking her home for a weekend, a huge airplane was heading toward the freeway in front of us. It most likely had engine trouble, and the pilot was attempting to land. Instantly, I froze, not knowing whether to brake or accelerate! For that moment, I knew my life was over. At the last second, the plane veered upward above the trees and out of sight.

Experience on Route 71

While heading north on Route 71,
I saw an airplane approaching the freeway.
I shouted to my wife, that it was descending,
And was about to crash into us that day.

My heart rapidly began to pound,
Since there was no escape left or right.
I did not know whether to speed up or brake,
And we in the car held our breath with fright.

There was a man in front of our auto
Who on a motorcycle was riding.
I know he thought this moment was his end,
As he discerned his life was subsiding.

That plane seemed to have a motor problem,
With no place except the freeway to land.
When it came closer than fifty feet,
The pilot veered upward and regained command.

Since we were lucky to see the thing,
We learned that it was a huge army plane.
Why it was in trouble was never found out,
But thank God it did not land in our lane.

On another occasion, Lori had a word processor that needed repaired, so she could finish her term papers. Since Jeffery worked for an airline company, I was able to fly free to Columbus and bring it back to Cleveland to be repaired. As I was waiting for the return flight in the terminal, I heard that all flights to the east were cancelled because of severe weather. The clouds over the airport were ominously black.

Strangely, the plane that I boarded to Cleveland was allowed to take off. The sunshine was absolutely gorgeous, as we flew above the clouds, but halfway to Cleveland, the plane flew into rainy and horribly windy conditions. It bounced through the turbulence like a toy. How thankful I was, when I saw the terminal tower building below and we landed safely! As I exited the plane, a woman walking next to me shouted, "Where is the nearest bathroom? I will never fly in one of those small planes again." That plane had twenty-nine seats. The word processor was totally smashed, and a new one had to be purchased in order for her to complete the requirements.

CHAPTER 12

Transition in the Nineties and the New Millennium

On January 17, 1992, our family celebrated Joy's mother's seventy-fifth birthday by flying as a family to Disney World in Florida. What a joyous occasion, as we left the snow and bitter cold in Ohio! Before that trip, I had only been to Florida in August of 1969, when the temperature was near one hundred degrees, for my brother-in-law's wedding. Even though this trip was in January, it was still incredible, when we exited the plane in Orlando, and felt the seventy-five-degree warmth.

Outside our motel, the swimming pool was open, but we could not leap into the southern water, because we had not taken our swimming suits.

We spent our first full day in Florida at the Disney theme park. On television, I had occasionally seen the Christmas parades on Disney Boulevard. What a different perception I had: I had thought the place was a city!

Because my mother-in-law was wheelchair bound, we could enter most of the rides without waiting in long lines.

She was terribly afraid of heights. Near the conclusion of the day, I convinced her to go with our family on the cable car that traveled across the park. At the halfway point of the ride, there was an electrical glitch. The ride stopped, leaving us dangling in the darkness for about a half hour. A woman in another car shouted an expletive, which I was convinced everyone in the entire park could hear!

Needless to say, my mother-in-law could have strangled me for convincing her to endure the experience.

The second day we spent at MGM. That sunny, seventy-five-degree weather of the day before, changed to monsoon-like rain. We had to purchase plastic raincoats to shield ourselves from being drenched, because we foolishly did not think about taking raincoats or umbrellas.

What a contrast, as we froze with a temperature of forty-nine degrees, and cuddled in the bleachers watching a live rendition of *Indiana Jones,* where the movie was produced!

I was impressed with the replica of the Empire State Building, which was so realistic that it could have been used in a movie or on television. Most actions are probably fakes, houses facades, and in-house activities transpiring in a studio.

After we browsed through the many souvenir shops, and bought memorabilia near closing time, we joined the crowd that took the ferry back to the parking lot.

One of my desires, before we left Florida, was to buy an orange tree and lemon tree. For some reason, the lemon tree never rooted, but that orange tree is still alive after seventeen years. Too bad the mini-oranges are not edible, but the blossoms smell delightful.

The morning of January 20, we boarded a huge airbus. The weather cleared, and we were ready for the flight to Cleveland. The cloudless sky seemed like a fitting conclusion to a wonderful-birthday celebration.

Because we were assigned to first class for the flight home, we were provided with a full-course meal. Within ten minutes into the flight, the attendant began to take food orders. Just before we indicated our choice of food, we heard and felt a huge boom! Instantly, the plane was slanting toward the earth.

Nervously, I said to Joy, "We are in trouble!"

Abruptly, the pilot informed us, that the plane had just blown one of its two engines, and that we should prepare for an emergency landing in Jacksonville Airport, where he believed we would land safely, though the airport is not equipped for huge aircraft. I knew that we would instantly be in heaven, especially when we were instructed to put our heads between our legs upon landing. To the man who sat behind me, I handed a gospel tract, and said that I hope he had accepted Jesus Christ as his Savior, because I thought this life was over.

"If you notice," he exclaimed, "the ocean has no white caps. The pilot can land this plane in the ocean, and we can slide down a chute to be rescued."

What a horrible sight I saw, as we neared the airport! Through the window, I could see numerous emergency vehicles and their flashing red lights!

In spite of our plight, the people remained calm!

As I sat nervously, I wondered how in the world we could be on a plane that had blown an engine, and most likely was about to crash. Miraculously, the pilot brought the plane to a grinding stop.

When the plane arrived at the terminal at noon, we had to remain in our seats for nearly a half hour, because of the smoking rubber on the wheels.

The passengers immediately formed a line to thank the pilot for a safe landing.

From there, some headed to the bar to drink themselves drunk.

The Near Tragedy over Florida

In the month of January 1992,
My family boarded a plane to Ohio
After a pleasant two days in Disney,
South of the city of Orlando.

As our family sat strapped to our seats,
We heard words in case of an emergency.
But since flying is the safest mode to roam,
We hoped there would be no such urgency.

After the wait on the lengthy runway,
The two-engine jet was ready for liftoff.
As we nervously gazed out of the windows,
We were eventually rising aloft.

About ten minutes into our journey,
We instantly heard a loud, jolting boom.
The attendants, who were serving the dinner,
Looked like they thought we were doomed.

Dennis R. Fox

The huge plane had risen above the ocean
To more than thirty-two thousand feet.
The hair upon my head shot upward
As I stared, imprisoned in my seat.

The direction we had once been pointing
Was no longer parallel ahead.
As we glanced toward the horizon,
We all believed we soon would be dead.

Those words uttered by the flight attendant
Suddenly took on a crippling meaning.
We knew our moments on earth were numbered
While incredibly no one was screaming.

We were advised to listen to the pilot,
Who wanted us to believe we were secure.
He calmly uttered, "The plane blew an engine,
But in Jacksonville, we'll not crash for sure."

He tried to give us that assurance
While some clutched booze and began to drink.
An optimist who was sitting behind me
Said we could land in the ocean and not sink.

Since I knew my next step was heaven,
A gospel tract I handed to that man.
I told him I hoped he knew his destiny
And that the direction to Christ was in his plan.

As we glided closer to the airport,
We were advised to take false teeth out.
All watches and jewels we placed in our pockets,
Along with other loose items about.

As we approached the short landing strip,
We had to tuck our heads between our knees.
Quickly, I glanced out the clouded window
And saw flashing lights beyond the trees.

But it wasn't God's time for us to join Him
As the one good engine powered us to a stop.
For a half hour, we sat in silence.
Thankfully, the other one did not flop.

After we experienced that ordeal
And entered the terminal that afternoon,
The passengers formed a line, where the pilot sat
And thanked him that our end did not come too soon.

I often wonder why we were not killed
When I hear of a similar story.
Then I realize it was not in God's plan,
And for that, I must give Him the glory.

The plane we were taking to Newark needed some windows replaced, because upon its landing, they had been smashed by birds. How Joy and I were lucky enough to board another plane with a problem was amazing to us! At seven thirty that evening, we boarded the plane that took us to Newark Airport. In flight, we could see the Washington Monument from a distance, and as we flew over New York City, just before we landed, the sight of the millions of lights was breathtaking!

When we landed, we learned that we had missed the last plane of the day to Cleveland by five minutes, and had to spend the night in a hotel. How grateful we were to the Lord, though, for a safe trip home!

As I approached June 1995 and had taught more than thirty years, I contemplated completing thirty-five, because I would have received a retirement benefit of 88 percent of my salary. My thought was that I could manage to teach a little more than three years and take advantage of that benefit.

In the Cleveland school system, teachers could accumulate unused sick days, of which I had many banked. Normally, one retiring was paid 30 percent of the unused days.

That year, teachers with more than thirty years were offered a one-time separation pay of 40 percent, but their retirement had to be accomplished before April 1. After that, the pay would be 30 percent.

The art teacher who taught next door to where I taught and knew that I had over thirty years, said that I should take advantage of the deal, and that I would not regret a positive move.

Because of his advice, I drove to the retirement board in Columbus, signed the papers, took them to the board of education, and officially retired on July 1, 1995. Even though I had many wonderful teaching experiences, gained volumes of beautiful student memories and the friendship of colleagues, and had great feedback from former students, I knew the timing was right!

Before 1995, the only phones that I knew existed were line, cordless, and automobile phones. After I made the decision to retire, a salesman came to Lincoln to offer the teachers a cell phone deal. As I listened to his presentation, I became so impressed with the idea of a phone I could attach to my belt or put into my pocket, that I signed a contract-and also became convinced that I could sell those contracts.

At the conclusion of that meeting, I told him about my coming retirement and my wish to work for his employer. Without hesitation, he set a day and time for an interview. At that interview, I was hired. What timing, because the next week I was available to attend five eight-hour paid training sessions, since it was during Easter vacation!

By the end of the training period, a number of us in the sessions became convinced we would do extremely well, since cell phones were relatively new to Northeast Ohio, and really seemed like a tremendous business opportunity. Selling five required contracts a week did not seem unreasonable, but the representative indicated, even before we started the door knocking, that we were fortunate, if we sold one out of every one hundred contacts made. That statement should have been an omen!

At that time, one signed a contract for a phone. A credit check was made, before the customer could sign an agreement. If one had unsatisfactory credit, he had to pay a security deposit of $300 to $1,000, depending upon how low his credit score was, but earned 6 percent interest as long as the customer possessed the phone. Needless to say, if one had poor credit, he most likely did not have the cash for the deposit and was unable to have the phone.

Also, if the phone were lost, stolen, or damaged, the customer was responsible for paying for a replacement.

I learned quickly, how difficult it was to be a salesman. There were four people at a business establishment who wanted phones. After presenting the plan, not one person signed a contract! One had the worst credit rating, another did not have a driver's license, and the other two had financial problems.

There was an educator, who I knew was a guaranteed sale, but that person also had bad credit and was not eligible to sign a contract.

Another family wanted cell phones to replace the landline phones, thinking money could be saved, but they too had financial problems and were denied.

Daily, I became enslaved to the new challenge, and most of the time was discouraged by hearing the word *no*. I struggled to try to reach quotas by working on Memorial Day, the Fourth of July, Saturdays, and Sundays. On those blistering hot days of June and July, I faithfully hung flyers on doors and made follow-up calls.

Totally I sold twenty-nine contracts, which fell well below the requirement, and was terminated in the middle of July.

In the meantime, I thought about what employment I would seek. Joy suggested that since I was experienced in education, I should look into subbing. I was not thrilled about that idea but unenthusiastically took her advice, and headed east on Interstate 90 to the Cleveland Board of Education. In fact, my intuition was to cease heading in that direction, because I figured more than thirty-one years in the classroom was enough, and really did not wish to deal with the headaches substitutes face.

Momentarily, there seemed to be a voice telling me to continue the drive.

As I stepped into the personnel office, a friendly secretary greeted me. When I indicated that I had retired in June and wished to substitute in the high schools, she handed me an application, and I was immediately hired.

I imagined that as a substitute, I would be greeted by horrible experiences. The very first assignment was for a mathematics teacher at John Marshall High School. Shock! Every class that day treated me with respect! What a great beginning!

For the next ten years, I began to know many of the young people and teachers at John Marshall and Max Hayes Vocational School. Because I had good rapport with them, numerous teachers requested me weekly as their substitute.

There were students who challenged my authority, but because I had learned how to communicate with students, carried a cell phone, and had direct communication with the administration, disruptions were kept to a minimum.

There was one student to whom I refused entrance to the class, because he was late, and there was a school lockout, when the bell rang. In retaliation, he punched his fist into the door window. A security guard was in the vicinity and escorted him away! He learned a bloody, hand-cut lesson!

The Lord always provided me with jobs, where there was a piano. That was true at Lincoln Junior High School, Max Hayes, and John Marshall. At John Marshall, there was an unused storage closet, where I moved a decent upright piano, and could practice and write original music during the hours I had no classes.

I had assignments when I did not need to instruct. Teachers had well-prepared lesson plans, and once the assignments were explained, I was able to write music and poetry.

One day I wrote a poem called "Crows." I asked one of the English instructors to read the finished copy, and that teacher advised me to continue poetry writing. Because of the encouragement of many students, teachers, and church members, I completed over two hundred religious and secular poems.

Crows

Hundreds of crows descended upon gigantic trees.
In the moonlight, they were seen by naked eyes.
They owned those limbs at which they clutched.
The screech they made caught all by surprise.

From the highest branches, those black beasts made their point.
The song they sang was heard from many a yard.
The silence of the night was shattered by loud thunder
As they flapped their wings and stood their guard.

One Christmas season, while I was a member of Mid-Brook Baptist Church, I began to think about the millions of lights that are strung on trees, houses, and lawns throughout the world. Tradition, Santa Claus, beauty, and the creation of excitement for children are some of the reasons for the displays, but I also know that millions do it to celebrate the birth of our Lord Jesus Christ.

Thinking about the lights prompted me to write an arrangement called "Christmas Lights."

Upon its completion, I gave it to the music director of the Mid-Brook choir with the potential that the choir would sing it. She and the pastor agreed that the words were somewhat worldly.

So shocked and upset I was with their responses, that I read the words to my mother-in-law, who I knew would agree with me.

After she read it, she said, "Why don't you revise it?"

Instead of self-pity, since three adult believers disagreed with the words, I analyzed what I had written. In less than an hour, I changed the words. When my mother-in-law read the new lyrics, she said, "Now it is biblical!"

A schoolteacher read the revised words and agreed that the change had been necessary.

When he finished reading it, I said, "I do not know what to call it."

Without hesitation, he said, "Call it 'Christmas Redemption.'"

As I continue to live, I find it miraculous that communicating with friends and family, having an open mind, and having changed what I thought at first was professional, have all led me down a more proficient path so many times. This, of course, was one example, and because I listened to others, that song has been enjoyed for years!

The first page of "Christ Redemption"

How could anyone forget September 11, 2001? The day began with the sun shining brightly, a typical September morning in Cleveland.

138

I was in John Marshall subbing an art class. Just as the students were changing classes after first period and the next class was entering the room, a student turned on the television set.

It was forbidden without permission for any student to tamper with the televisions in any room. Immediately and dogmatically, I instructed him to shut it off.

Abruptly, he told me that one of the Twin Towers in New York City was on fire. With that news, I reversed my decision and told him to keep it on.

As the moments elapsed, we learned the horrific news as it developed throughout the day. How tortuous it was to watch the two towers implode and see the frightened mob attempt to escape the gush of debris!

To compound the agony, we learned that America was continuing to be attacked by aircraft as a plane slammed into the Pentagon and another one crashed into a Pennsylvania hillside, most likely bound for the Capitol in Washington but thwarted by brave people.

On Friday, September 21, I again was subbing at John Marshall High School. An office clerk who knew I had written poetry, asked me just before I entered a class, if I intended to write a poem about 9-11.

"No way," I said.

Momentarily, I thought, *How could I write a poem about such a horrible event, especially in light of the fact that I was not near the catastrophe?*

Into that class I entered. After I handed out the assignment, words began to formulate in my mind. By the time the class period ended, I had created three stanzas.

Weeks later, I was sitting in a hospital waiting room and had just completed the final verse. In total excitement, I told a woman sitting next to me, that I had just finished the final line of a poem about 9-11 and wanted to know, if she wished to hear it.

Without hesitation, she said, "Yes!"

When I finished reading it, I said, "I have a problem. I do not know what to call it."

A man sitting nearby who I did not think was paying attention to my reading left his seat and said, "Call it 'Freedom under Fire.'"

To myself, I thought, *Bingo! That is it!*

Not long after the poem was completed, I saw the same secretary heading from the parking lot to her workstation. Ebulliently, I said, "I have in my hands the completed 9-11 poem."

She said, "Please, read it now!"

At the conclusion, she said, "As you were reading, I felt as though I were there; it was horribly realistic. Send it to Tom Brokaw and quickly develop it into a musical composition."

I took her surprising advice (not sending it to Mr. Brokaw), and perhaps six months later, I completed the original musical draft.

A bass singer from a local church read the poem at a piano recital of my students while I played the musical rendition.

My wish has been to have it sung during the yearly program at the site in New York.

Freedom Under Fire

It was a crystal-blue sky on that Tuesday morn.
People went about their business, as was their norm.
Travelers boarded their planes with different plans to do.
But on four of those jets, hijackers overtook the crew.

Little children and adults were in fear as they sped.
In that moment, they feared they would soon be dead.
Outside those cabin walls, the US did not know
That a terrible news flash would suddenly flow.

Two of those planes would slam into the New York Twin Towers.
Nations were about to relive the news for many hours.
Little did the world know, it was in for more horrible shock
When a third plane crashed into the Pentagon block.

Flying across PA, a fourth plane was doomed,
For into the earth those passengers became entombed.
As those victims were faced with the enemy's plot,
Brave ones fought those barbarians right on the spot.

As Americans watched the horror of the sight,
We learned those planes had become missiles in flight,
For upon the television screen, we looked in despair,
Viewing with disbelief the demonic affair!

When those two towers imploded to the street,
We feared thousands would die from the intense heat.
Firemen rushed to rescue as many as they could
But were crushed by debris, where most of them stood.

One wonders why those monsters in the prime of life
Would learn to abhor freedom with such brutal strife?
Ruthlessly, they commandeered those airlines we possess,
Cunningly murdering lives with condemned success!

Those culprits who masterminded that vicious deed
Must be apprehended and punished with lightning speed!
President Bush was dogmatic with his instant plan
To destroy them as quickly as we can!

What they aspired to accomplish forever
Was to wipe out our freedom in their endeavor!
But they were messing with a united force,
And that kind of assault we must never endorse!

The atrocity that they inflicted that day
Brought multitudes of people to their knees to pray.
They asked God to bless the government of our great land,
Raising the stars and stripes while united we stand!

This nation has fought to keep the freedom throughout the years.
It will not allow miscreants to control our fears.
Pilgrims settled here with religious freedom on their minds
And prayed we would not be conquered!
We will not be conquered!
We will not be conquered!
We will not be conquered by the hostile kind!

141

At this juncture, the professional reproduction is not available.

On August 29, 1998, Michael and Kristie were married in her parents' front yard near Vermillion, Ohio, along the shore of Lake Erie.

For the ceremony, Kristie's sister played a flute solo, and I accompanied her at the keyboard.

A multimillionaire who developed the suspended ceilings and his wife lived in the mansion on the adjacent property. For a wedding gift, they gave Mike, Kristie, and six of us from the wedding party a ride in his jet copter along the shore of Lake Erie from Vermillion to Sandusky, north of the Cedar Point amusement park.

On the return flight, I looked below just before we landed and saw a huge heart etched into the sandy beach with Michael and Kristie's names. What a beautiful sight, just before we delved into the food and they unwrapped their gifts!

Michael and Kristie

My daughter, Lori; sons Jeff and Michael; mother-in-
law Dorothy; Joy; and yours truly next to Lake Erie

Since then, Joy and I have been blessed with two beautiful
grandchildren, Kayla and Abbey, who have become the apples of our
eyes.

Joy and I babysat them from birth, while their mother and dad
worked.

Every summer, they enjoyed swimming in Grandma and Grandpa's
swimming pool, where they and their cousins learned to swim.

My desire is that in time they master the piano as their grandpa did.

We continuously played the CD *Veggie Tales* with gospel songs and
choruses. Kayla learned to sing most of them from memory. For her
great-grandmother's ninetieth birthday party, she sang "O How I Love
Jesus" with my accompaniment, when she was only five years old before
about fifty adults.

Kayla spent preschool and kindergarten at the Montessori School
in Westlake, Ohio. On her last day, we attended the annual promotion
ceremony. While we sat, Jeffery called to surprise us that he and Aubrey
had just married in a private ceremony. Because of that wedding, they
added a stepchild, Isaac, to our family.

Jeff and Aubrey

I love you Grandma and Grandpa Fox, and your pool! Merry Christmas Love, Isaac

Isaac and his creativity

It is very important that those children receive a Christian education. The girls are going to the Church of the Open Door in Elyria, Ohio, which teaches that through the blood of Jesus Christ and accepting Him as Savior, one goes to heaven.

On three separate instances in 1998 and 1999, I became very ill and nearly passed out. Within one hour of the episode, I returned to normal. I thought it was the flu, but after the third episode, Joy advised me to see the doctor.

A heart specialist in the Cleveland Clinic ordered me to have a test to determine why the episode occurred. The test concluded that I have vasovagal syncope, a problem with the main nerve in the body that can cause one to become violently ill at any time.

Because of that test, he ordered me to have my heart monitored for twenty-four hours three weeks apart. The first test unfortunately revealed that my heart was pausing three seconds at a time. On the second test, it was pausing ten seconds at a time.

On July 8, 1999, the doctor placed a pacemaker into my chest. Had it not been for the original test, the electrical problem to my heart would not have been discovered. It was all in God's hands!

During the years that Joy and I were members of Mid-Brook, I played the piano the last Sunday of the month. I happened to be the player when an evangelist was holding a meeting. As the congregation was singing one of the songs, he abruptly stopped the singing, looked at me, and asked if I knew Lee Baum.

I was in complete shock!

"He was my piano teacher at Piedmont Bible College over forty years ago," I said.

"Your technique," he said, "is just like his."

The fact that I had never met that evangelist before that service and that he could compare our techniques was an astounding coincidence!

The Unbelievable Connection

When I was in Bible college,
I took piano lessons
From music Professor Lee H. Baum
For four years of weekly sessions.

I was playing the piano
Virtually forty years later
During an evening service
When we had a guest minister.

Abruptly, he stopped the order
Of the singing service that day
And asked me, if I ever heard
A man named Lee H. Baum play.

At that moment, I was struck with shock
When that surprising question was asked,
For he had connected my technique to his
After those many years had passed!

What was also astonishing is that
Throughout the last forty long years,
Neither the guest preacher nor I
With him had contact by eyes or ears!

It was not long before an interest in some of my gospel choruses and choral arrangements occurred.

That interest really grew when I received a call from Marilyn, a former member of the Madison Avenue Baptist Church and an attendee of Mid-Brook. She asked me, if I would harmonize two original gospel hymns that she had written. I do not make it a policy to harmonize other writers' melody lines, but I indicated that I would see what she had written and give her an answer.

Unknown to her, one of the song's melodies was already copyrighted, but I asked if she would want me to develop it into an original composition.

She accepted that idea, which began a massive musical project.

In 1988, Marilyn contracted ALS (Lou Gehrig's disease). Most who become afflicted with that deadly disease die within a year! She beat the odds and survived ten years after her diagnosis. I really believe that the Lord sustained her life for what lay ahead.

By the time she and I began to develop our ideas, she was totally bedridden, was kept alive with a breathing machine, and could not move any part of her body.

Before she was afflicted with that disease, her neighbors asked her to keep watch over their home, while they were on vacation. In that house, she saw a mouse, which created the idea in her mind to develop a humorous poem about the creature. The Lord used that incident to inspire her to write gospel poems.

In fact, from that day, even though the disease crippled her body, she mentally constructed 116 poems, before she was ushered into heaven in

1998. Imprisoned in bed with no motor movement except the blinking of her eyes and capable of only barely understood garbled speech, she would labor to dictate to her daughter and husband fifteen to twenty lines at a time with near poetic and rhythmic perfection. That skill in itself was a gift from the Lord.

I then created original musical scores from most of those poems. Within two or three months, the first three numbers were computerized.

The Plain Dealer newspaper in Cleveland learned about Marilyn's situation and our ability to write those hymns, and printed stories about our hymns and her condition on four different days. The first one was published on the front page on Sunday, July 2, 1995.

An article was also published in the *Akron Beacon Journal*.

Channel Five in Cleveland did a ten-minute story narrated by newscaster Ten Henry.

A major television station in New York City featured us in a morning program.

I was not totally satisfied with the gospel songs and hymns, when they were initially self-published into four volumes. I informed Marilyn that some of those hymns could be developed as choral arrangements. That began another major challenge. To this day, over ten choral arrangements from those songs have been perfected, with more in development. "Holy Night" (not the same as the popular "O Holy Night") was sung by the 150-member-John Marshall Concert Choir in Cleveland.

The first page of "Holy Night"

Nearly 2,500 of the songbooks have been sold throughout seventeen states. Another song that the late Pastor Hussey, the pastor of the Madison Avenue Baptist Church in Cleveland, said was really an outstanding inspiration was "In the Shadow of the Cross." That song, which is in volume one of the four *These Are Written That Ye Might Believe, John 20:31* songbooks, I composed into a choral arrangement, and it was sung by the Westlake Baptist Church Choir.

In the Shadow of the Cross

The first page of "In the Shadow of the Cross"

Since the books were selling quite well, I called the choir director of the Cleveland Baptist Church to tell him about our fundamentally Bible-based hymnbook called *These Are Written, That Ye Might Believe, John 20:31*. He agreed to peruse the book. That appointment with him opened the next opportunity in my life.

He said that one of his predecessors lived very close to the church and might be interested in purchasing the book.

I wasted no time in calling him, and during an office visit, he bought three copies of volume one and suggested that I meet him at a Baptist church in North Ridgeville for the Ohio Baptist Buckeye Fellowship pastors' and music directors' monthly meeting the following Tuesday to share how biblically based and professional the book is.

There were about seventy-five in attendance at that meeting.

As a result of my going to that conference, I began to receive a monthly bulletin telling where the next meetings were to be held.

The next one occurred at the Rocky River Baptist Church in Rocky River, Ohio, which was located only three miles from my home.

I called that pastor and let him know about the gospel hymnbook. During that visit, he wasted no time in inviting me to the next Buckeye meeting.

One of the songs that I introduced was "In the Shadow of the Cross." What a blessing it was to hear fifty or more men of God lift their voices as they sang that hymn!

When Pastor Males Sr.'s son heard that song and my accompaniment on the piano keys, he said at the conclusion of the service that he wanted his daughter to start taking piano lessons, even though he lived more than twenty-five miles from me.

Some months later, his wife and son also started to take lessons.

Every so often, she would tell me the need Rocky River Baptist had for a qualified choir director.

For years, the members of the church prayed that the Lord would provide them with someone who could build a musical program with songs that proclaim the messages of Jesus Christ.

In time, I decided to visit Rocky River Baptist on a Sunday morning to determine if it were the Lord's will for Joy and me to make the move.

As I sat in that service, I knew there was a need, with only eight choir members who sang only melodies and had no director.

After a meeting, Pastor Males Sr., the church, my wife, and I agreed that it was the Lord's will for us to join Rocky River Baptist and bring quality biblical music for the Lord. On the first Sunday of October 2001, I accepted the challenge to become the director.

The church's commitment has been not to compromise by preaching what God's Word says and not to lower the spiritual standard of their music program. It was my commitment that the music would bring glory to Jesus Christ, point the lost to Him, and introduce music with biblical and inspirational impact.

There are many churches today that are doing away with the good old gospel songs that were written by such authors as Fanny Crosby, Bill Gaither, and John W. Peterson. The hymnals with the praise songs and hymns are being replaced by repetitive phrases that have a beat but lack the meat of God's Word.

At the first rehearsal, I gave my testimony, and shared what I believed were appropriate plans that would give honor to our Lord.

When I began the next rehearsal, I had a preconceived idea that the members could read music and that I could approach rehearsals with the same format that I had used at the Madison Avenue Baptist Church. Surprise! Madison members could read music, and most of the sixteen members sang solos. Hardly anyone in Rocky River could read music or sing solos. All they sang were the melodies.

The Madison choir was already organized into the four sections of vocal range when I became the assistant director. The first order of singing at Rocky River was to establish the singer's vocal ranges. Those who were placed in the alto, tenor, or bass sections had to learn to harmonize.

The choir rapidly grew to nineteen members with five sopranos, five altos, four tenors, and five basses. How gratifying it was to hear them harmonize four-part gospel songs and choral arrangements, and to hear the development of beautiful tones and understood words!

During my first two years, they would sit with their families, until it was time for the specials to be sung. At that time, they would go to the pulpit area, stand while they sang, and return to their seats, which was time consuming and distracting.

Because the choir numbers increased, the pastor and church decided, it was time for a choir loft to be constructed with comfortable chairs. What a difference that made for professionalism and convenience for rehearsals and church services!

The Lord continued to bless in an unexpected way. I suggested that in time the church would need to consider purchasing an organ. Just after the choir loft and pulpit area were completed, Cleveland Baptist Church *gave* the church an organ that was not needed and just like new. What a difference that made to have both organ and piano played for the services!

Rocky River Baptist has had a number of ministries, such as passing out advertising flyers, witnessing in the neighborhoods, supporting missionaries, having missionary and Bible conferences, providing baptismal services for new converts, offering new convert classes to teach biblical principles, planning young peoples' activities, raising a benevolent fund, holding picnics, throwing anniversary dinners, and fellowshipping, and establishing nursery home ministries. Numerous times they have sung for the Ohio Buckeye Fellowship meetings, at a local mall, almost every Christmas at two nursing homes, and joined with another church in uplifting spiritual musical concerts.

Since I have continuously played the piano for the church services, others in the congregation have started to take lessons. Some have accompanied the choir, played in the song services, and played solos. There should not be a lack of pianists for years to come!

Recently, I attended the funeral of one of my former Madison Avenue Baptist Church choir members. His son-in-law asked all those who had sung my chorus "But These Are Written, John 20:31" to come forward and join in singing that song that has left an impact, wherever it has been sung. Over thirty from as far back as the 1960s lifted their voices in singing that song!

Throughout the years, members of Madison Avenue Baptist, Mid-Brook Baptist, and Rocky River Baptist (now Westlake Baptist) have urged me to send the choral arrangements to publishers. Three members of Westlake Baptist believed the arrangements should no longer be sung only locally and have produced letters that I should send to publishers. Since they gave me permission to include the letters in this book, I will let them speak for themselves!

The first letter comes from the former Rocky River Baptist pastor.

April 4, 2005

To whom it may concern:

I am sending this letter to let you know about the outstanding fundamental music written by our music director, Dennis Fox, and sung by our choir at the Rocky River Baptist Church, Rocky River, Ohio, where I am the pastor. The choir has had the privilege to sing some of those songs. All of his gospel arrangements proclaim the deity of our Lord Jesus Christ with messages of hope for those outside of Christ and inspiration for born-again believers. They certainly have had an enormous impact in my life and the lives of our choir and congregation.

The gospel music that I have heard on the radio and television and that is sung in many churches throughout the world over the last number of years has been geared basically toward contemporary flavor with a strong beat, repetitive phrases, and very little message, if any. The arrangements that he has written have the most important ingredient—the Word of God-but in addition, they have beautiful melodies and harmonies that I believe will be enjoyed by churches throughout the United States and beyond.

What joyous news it would be to the many who have heard the power that these songs contain if they were finally published and available to the world! Thank you for your careful perusal of them, as many pastors and I in the Ohio Buckeye Fellowship already have done.

A pastor who preaches God's Word,
Pastor Paul Males Sr.

This next letter came from member of the Rocky River Baptist Church choir.

March 22, 2005

To whom it may concern:

I am a choir member of the Rocky River Baptist Church. Our choir director is Dennis Fox, who has introduced us to at least eight choral numbers that he has written and that we have sung since he has been our director, with many more yet to be sung. The main purpose of that music has been to prepare the hearts and minds of all who are in our worship service to receive the Word of God. In every service, there are diverse ages and ethnic and financial backgrounds. That music has been the strain that has connected us together to focus on the message. It glorifies the Lord, shares testimonies, exhorts, and challenges the listener to look into his own heart so that he or she can say, "I can have that beautiful relationship." His music complements the message and makes the service complete. It contains fundamental truths that the Bible teaches and challenges us to meet a high moral standard based upon the Word of God.

There is a tremendous amount of music being sung in many religious organizations whose content is shallow and that just has a satisfying beat and repetitive phrases.

The songs that the Lord has permitted him to write not only do what I indicated, but also have beauty and are uplifting.

I pray that these renditions can become published, known, and sung, inspire, and impact thousands as they have the members of our church.

Yours in Christ,
Sachiko Krieger

The third letter was written by a member of Rocky River Baptist, who has sung some of my hymns and has preached in numerous churches in the United States.

May 1, 2005

Dear publisher:

I am a member of the Rocky River Baptist Church and an instructor of church history and the Bible at the Heritage Baptist Institute in Cleveland, Ohio. For a number of years, I have had the privilege of hearing the Rocky River Baptist Church Choir sing a number of profound, fundamental, Bible-based, and beautifully inspiring choral arrangements written by the choir director, Dennis Fox. It is satisfying to me to know that he is sending these worshipful choral songs for publication.

Throughout the years, I have sung solos and preached in many churches in the United States. I am convinced that there are scores of churches that lack good, sound biblical choral renditions or would add them to their library once they were heard. The songs written by Dennis would provide music for church services that is based upon Scripture and would prepare audiences for the most important part of the service: the message from God's Word. I would like nothing less than to learn that other churches will have the same opportunity our church has had for nearly four years to sing these well-constructed and professionally written songs.

Dennis and I know Jesus Christ as Savior and have the same desire for the world to know Him as we do. We believe that arrangements such as these will impact those who enter church services to say that between the message from God's Word, prayer, and the beauty of the choral numbers, they would return to the churches because they were blessed by all three and, if lost, find hope in the Lord Jesus Christ.

Yours in His Service,
Bruce Musselman

In 2007, Rocky River Baptist Church decided that a new direction was necessary. Because most of our members were not from the area, the congregation was too large for the size of the auditorium, and the Sunday school space was inadequate, it appeared to be the Lord's will that we sell the property and building and find a new location.

The Lord's will was confirmed, when three and a half acres of property on Bradley Road and one property north of Clemens Road in an outstanding location in Westlake, Ohio, became available for an unbelievable price at the same time our church was for sale. Another church bought our property for a little more than the cost of the new property, enabling us to pay off the Westlake property entirely!

Since a new building will have to be erected in time, a new facility needed to be found.

Again, we realized the Lord's leading, when the almost new Westlake Recreation Center offered us the meeting room in that facility for all of our services, a kitchen for social events, and nursery accommodations for affordable monthly payments with no additional cost for electric, heat, air-conditioning, or water.

An adjacent room with a sliding door is available for special events.

After the move was made, I had a concern that the choir would dissolve. There was no choir loft and no piano, and it was unclear, whether there would be enough people in the choir, since some of the members left the church for various reasons.

Much to my surprise, twelve choir members knew it was imperative to honor the Lord, by continuing to produce acceptable music, which is an important factor in the church's spiritual growth, is uplifting for congregational singing, provides a testimony for visitors, and constitutes a vital step before the messages.

A sixty-one-key keyboard was all we had since the church piano had to be stored until the new building would be constructed. The congregation agreed that an eighty-eight-keyboard was essential, and a new one was purchased.

With that keyboard, the choir continues to sing gospel songs and arrangements for Sunday services and has grown to fourteen members.

Not long after our church moved, Pastor Males Sr. retired and his son accepted the call from the Lord to become our pastor. He has a mission to do what his father did, and that is to preach and teach the Word, get everyone excited about our ministry, and to encourage all to read and study His Word, which is commanded in 2 Timothy 2:15 (KJV): "Study to shew thyself approved unto God, a workman that needeth not to be ashamed, rightly dividing the word of truth."

What is really important for our assembly is to witness new folks visiting our church, young people and adults accepting Christ as their Savior, being baptized, becoming workers in the church, and helping to spread the gospel to the neighborhoods!

In January of 2009, I was hired by the Heritage Baptist Institute, a ministry of Cleveland Baptist Church, to teach a musical directing course. Twenty-four men and ladies were in that class to learn about or increase their knowledge of the directing of choirs or congregational singing. Over half had no musical theory knowledge, which is almost necessary for one to know how to correct vocal problems, to organize a rehearsal, and to produce blended diction and harmony. By the end of the fifteen weeks, it was amazing to watch them skillfully direct gospel songs and arrangements, and hear some testify that they had started directing in their churches.

One of our members at Westlake Baptist Church became the congregational song leader three or four years ago without knowing the movements of a director. He and another member took that class, and both have worked diligently and are now using that skill.

In the years to come, if it is the Lord's will, I will continue to train younger people to sing, play the piano, direct congregational singing, and train choirs for His glory.

CHAPTER 13

Not the Final Chapter

Many times I have both heard and made this statement: "If I could do things differently, I would." I am not perfect, since I was born in sin according to God's Word and have been disobedient at times, but that is why 1 John 1:9-10 (KJV) is there for the believer who sins: "If we confess our sins, he is faithful and just to forgive us our sins, and to cleanse us from all unrighteousness. If we say that we have not sinned, we make him a liar, and his word is not in us." I believe that though I am not perfect, the Lord has given me a new life, since I accepted Him in 1952. What a joy it has been to study His Word and to share my faith since that day, and to see lost people accepting Christ, because of what Jesus Christ has done for me as a believer!

Throughout the years, I continued to tell segments of my life's experiences. After I accepted the challenge to become the choir director of what is now Westlake Baptist Church, the pastor asked me to give my testimony during the first rehearsal.

After that day, I came to the conclusion that it might be important to share in print how Christ saved me from a life of corruption and opened doors of Christian opportunities.

I told Pastor Males Sr. that when I was a youngster, I believed I was ignorant. That belief had a major impact on my early years, and by putting how wrong I was into print, I could be an inspiration to others, who have had similar discouragements.

He interrupted me and said, "Do not tell the readers that that is why you developed this autobiography. Tell them instead that you want them to know what Jesus Christ did in your life, and that their lives can be changed, if they accept Him as you did."

With his advice and encouragement, he told me not to stop until the task is finished. Even though this book is written, I titled this section "Not the Final Chapter."

At this juncture, my life is not over, and as I live, I hope to be a blessing and to witness the miracles of the Lord in my life and with those with whom I associate!

For those who read the pages of my autobiography and have not accepted the Lord Jesus as their Savior, it is not too late. Be assured, though, there is no guarantee about tomorrow. One can find the way to heaven by doing what the Bible says in John 1:12 (KJV): "But as many as received Him, to them gave he power to become the sons of God, even to them that believe on his name."

Because God's precious Word is real and contains the message of hope, and because He saved me when I was a teenager, I encourage all to make sure of their salvation and heaven, before it is eternally too late. In 2 Corinthians 2:6b (KJV), the apostle Paul gave us these important words: "Behold, now is the accepted time; behold now is the day of salvation."

Finally, I praise the Lord for directing me to the right people at the right times and places. Those were not accidental encounters. They were orchestrated by the Divine! At birth, I was not born into God's family, but once I was born again, I had the responsibility to serve Him by sharing my faith, so that hell does not need to be one's destination.

The Lord provided my path to a Christian wife, three great children, two daughters-in-law, two grandchildren, and a step-grandchild-but most of all, He granted me the honor of serving Jesus Christ, my eternal Savior!

After I had completed what I thought would be the last chapter of this book, my life was dramatically and unexpectedly altered. More than three years ago, Joy's blood pressure began to spike over 225, which really concerned the doctors and our families. Specialists ordered varied prescriptions to try to correct the problem.

After weeks, her blood pressure subsided to near normal, and we assumed she was out of the woods.

On April 11, 2012, her blood pressure problem reoccurred, but this time, her back and arms were in such tremendous pain that I took her to our nearby hospital.

Unfortunately, she was taken to the intensive care unit with a heart attack.

On April 16, she was ushered into heaven. How thankful I am for the comforting words to the believers from Paul in 2 Corinthians 5:8 (KJV), which says, "We are confident, I say, and willing rather to be absent from the body, and to be present with the Lord." I know we will be together in eternity!

Numerous times, she said that before she died, she wanted to visit our grandchildren's grandma and grandpa days at their school, the Open Door Christian School, in Elyria, Ohio, every year; see them graduate from high school and college; and celebrate our fiftieth wedding anniversary on September 21, 2013, with our church family and friends.

How wonderful it was to be married for forty-seven years to such a wonderful Christian wife, but I know she is in a better place and free of earthly sufferings!

Since Joy left our families, I began to reflect upon the impact she had on our lives at home, at church, and everywhere she communicated. How important it was that the Lord brought her into my life, not by accident, but by a divine encounter-a born-again believer who first saw me at her grandfather's funeral, where I had the privilege to lead a prayer at the gravesite.

How wonderful to recall our blessed years that we shared together: our wedding, our honeymoon to the New York Adirondack Mountains, the trips to her brother and family in Tennessee, our trip to celebrate my mother and father's fiftieth anniversary, our trip to Disney World to celebrate her mother's seventy-fifth birthday, the births of our children, the births of our grandchildren, and our babysitting them while their mother and father worked, the chance to see our children slide down dad's homemade toboggan slide and ice rink until the neighbor hood kids created dangerous ice balls, where my children and my grandchildren learned to swim and splash in our backyard swimming pool, grandpa's constructed ice rink, fishing trips, amusement parks, and celebrate Michael's, Jeff's, and Lori's graduation from high school and her graduation from Ohio State University. How she cherished making Thanksgiving and Christmas our celebration of joy with our children by decorating the nine-and-a-half-foot live Christmas trees that nearly touched our ceiling! I will always remember her enjoying making the season a joyous occasion by helping to buy gifts for all of our families, buying chocolate in abundance from Malley's candy stores, spending Saturdays shopping at the local stores, buying bushels of apples to make homemade applesauce and drink gallons of cider, traveling the gorgeous Metropolitan Park System in Cuyahoga County and taking in the view of Lake Erie every season, encouraging me as I worked to become Ohio certified, get my master's degree, and taught English and music for more than thirty years, sharing the good news of salvation with our neighbors, making it our obligation to be in a Christ-centered church *with our children* every week to learn the importance of accepting Christ and to live for Him, and standing beside me as we renewed our vows in August of 1988 in our yard. What a memory, as I sadly gander at the twenty yards of dirt that was just spread, where the four-by-eighteen-by-thirty-three-foot swimming pool and deck once stood, and at the handprints of our grandchildren, step-grandchild, Joy, Lori, and me from when she had us dip our hands into paint and place them on the wooden fence!

My wife, our two grandchildren, and me

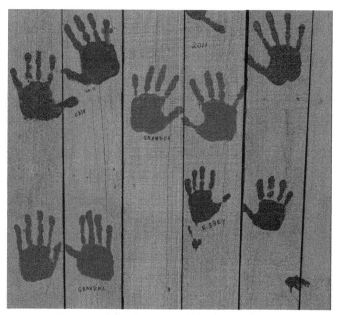

Picture of the fence with those handprints
Lori, my daughter, called Odie by our grandchildren,

Grandpa, Grandma,
Abbey, my grandchild

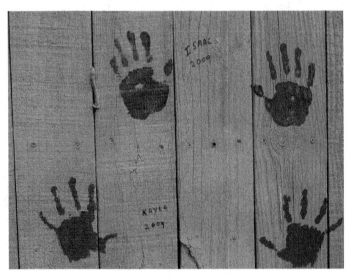

Isaac, my step-grandson,
Kayla, my grandchild

Super news arrived this summer when Kayla and her mother, Kristie, who trusted the Lord earlier, were baptized and Abbey accepted Jesus into her heart at a Christian camp. Unfortunately, Joy was not alive to learn about this great eternal news.

What better way to conclude what I have shared about my life than by my quoting Jude 24-25 (KJV), which was repeated on numerous occasions by the late Reverend Burtner at Camp Mt. Lou San after his encouraging messages to the campers: "Now unto him that is able to keep you from falling, and to present you faultless before the presence of his glory with exceeding joy, to the only wise God our Savior, be glory and majesty, dominion and power, both now and ever. Amen."

Available at dennisrobertfox@gmail.com

My professional CD recording of *Favorite Gospel Piano Arrangements*

1. When They Ring the Golden Bells
2. He Died for Me
3. There Is Power in the Blood
4. The Old Rugged Cross
5. O How I Love Jesus
6. Holy Ghost, with Light Divine
7. When the Roll is Called Up Yonder
8. Master, the Tempest Is Raging
9. He Lives
10. And Can It Be That I Should Gain?
11. Wonderful Peace
12. Grace Greater Than Our Sin
13. O That Will Be Glory
14. What a Friend We Have in Jesus

And the complete songs in *Born to Serve*

Printed in the United States
By Bookmasters